Your Towns and Cities in the

Leeds
in the Great War

To Joseph Schofield, who fought in the first war, and
helped rebuild London after the second

Your Towns and Cities in the Great War

Leeds
in the Great War

Stephen Wade

Pen & Sword
MILITARY

First published in Great Britain in 2016 by
PEN & SWORD MILITARY
an imprint of
Pen and Sword Books Ltd
47 Church Street
Barnsley
South Yorkshire S70 2AS

ISBN 978 1 47386 154 1

A CIP record for this book is available from the British Library.

Printed and bound in England
by CPI Group (UK) Ltd, Croydon, CR0 4YY

Typeset in Times New Roman

Pen & Sword Books Ltd incorporates the imprints of
Pen & Sword Archaeology, Atlas, Aviation, Battleground, Discovery,
Family History, History, Maritime, Military, Naval, Politics, Railways,
Select, Social History, Transport, True Crime, and Claymore Press,
Frontline Books, Leo Cooper, Praetorian Press, Remember When,
Seaforth Publishing and Wharncliffe.

For a complete list of Pen and Sword titles please contact
Pen and Sword Books Limited
47 Church Street, Barnsley, South Yorkshire, S70 2AS, England

E-mail: enquiries@pen-and-sword.co.uk
Website: **www.pen-and-sword.co.uk**

Contents

Introduction

Writing about the history of one's own home town is a peculiarly strange task; when the history in question is still just within the compass of oral history, or at least exists in the family myths and legends, then that strange feeling is enlarged and enriched by a process of enquiry that has to resist too much subjectivity. My preparation for the book consisted of a few random questions, a skimming of family photograph albums, and an interrogation of my own memory; after all, I had known and spoken to several survivors of the Great War.

What was for many years in my writing life merely another historical subject suddenly became partly an examination of my own preconceptions about that war and its aftermath.

Great historical events tend to generate myths along with the statistics, and sometimes these perhaps distorted tales penetrate family history. Such is the case with my Leeds family. The focus for this is an old photograph, showing my grandfather, Private Joseph Schofield, of the King's Own Yorkshire Light Infantry, standing between two uniformed Tommies. Was he the cook, as he was wearing a dull cream shirt and white trousers, or was he a prisoner of war? In my childhood, the questions bothered me for years, until one day I asked an uncle. Yes, it seems that Joe was a cook. That matched well with my childhood memories of visiting the Schofields in their Beeston terrace, as Granddad Joe would make me 'army porridge' or an 'army breakfast', which meant essentially food in lard and fried so that it was generally delicious – at a time when everything at meals seemed to be oily.

I was born in Leeds at St Margaret's Maternity Home on Hyde Park, just after the war with Hitler, and my earliest memories are run through with things military. Uncles from the Wade family in Churwell and Gildersome served in the navy, army and air force. Memories of the First World War, though, rarely came up; the second war dominated talk, as I heard about the siege of Malta and life on minesweepers. Why was the Great War so marginal? I didn't ask this question until I was in my twenties. But I have asked it since, particularly when I learned about Dr Peter Liddle of Ripon, who set about capturing Great War memories, realizing that they were being lost to the oblivion of textless history.

Today, approaching the subject of the contributions of Leeds to that war, and the experience of local people on the home front as well as in the theatres of war across Europe and Asia, I feel a sense of duty in reclaiming some of the stories. There was a long, uneasy silence in the interwar years regarding some of the sheer enormity of the loss of life in a war whose nature had never been created before, throughout the long chronicle of the British Empire.

Of course, there is already a vast literature on the subject, and that doyen of Leeds writers, soaked in local memories, Alan Bennett, has in a sense given all future Leeds memoirists a template for the Great War family story. This is in his essay *Uncle Clarence*, in which he recounts a trip to find the war grave of his uncle, who died in Flanders on 21 October 1917. Bennett neatly isolates the iconic nature of all our glorious dead in that conflict by writing, 'He was always twenty all through my childhood …' I feel exactly that when I look at Private Joseph Schofield. Although he survived the war, and I got to know him as a warm, friendly grandfather in the 1950s, he was, in another strange way, also frozen in time in that photo, and that was from a war that meant nothing to me and my family cousins, not until we were older and had been educated about the family past – though even then it was never direct and accessible.

Bennett makes it clear that his Uncle Clarence was a presence also, in the same way that those who died nobly are always there, always revered. He writes, 'Clarence, later a silly-ass kind of name, a name out of farce and like Albert, never re-vamped, remains in our family the name of a saint.' This is further explained by a memory of my own, as I sat in the graveyard at Stanbury, near Howarth, studying the war memorial. A woman arrived in a car and we chatted. It transpired that her great-uncle was listed on that stone of dignity and respect, another death in the long list from the Western Front. She visited his memorial, along with her mother's grave, and as I left she said she would go and have a chat with them. It is, of course, a one-way dialogue – a monologue technically, but in our imaginations, they speak. The endless silence of their going leaves a need to create words and to speak with their shades.

The Great War was like no other. People everywhere sensed that this was a war with unimagined dimensions, and as they read the first accounts of the assassination of Archduke Franz Ferdinand by Serbian Gavrilo Princip, followed by the dominos going over as state followed state in having bonds and allegiances with neighbours or with other allies, the sheer horror of the coming conflict was apparent. Then followed the call to arms and Lord Kitchener's appeal for his 'new armies'. The scale of the sacrifice demanded was not really grasped for some time: the first confrontations, with their heavy death tolls, gave a sense of terrible foreboding, and the general chatter about the war being over by Christmas faded as the Pals and Chums battalions went to their lengthy training periods at the camps of the Northern and Southern Commands. In Leeds's case, the Pals were headed for Colsterdale in North Yorkshire.

That war is also like no other from the writer's point of view. It presents the major problem of being so gargantuan that chipping out a local narrative from that great block of history is a bit like a sculptor trying to imagine the finished figure before any part of the work is decided on. The writer knows roughly what the spine of the narrative is, and he or she knows the city in question, but from multiple stories come the ones that are to define the angle that the writer takes on the subject.

In this case, it was not simply a matter of selection and rejection of material; it was far more. In truth, it was a voyage of discovery for me. Readers will be aware that often one's own town is the least familiar; we tend to take more notice of the strange. When we arrive somewhere new we see details, we read footnotes, we absorb slowly. Strangely, when we grow up in a place, we look past and beyond strands of important matters. Familiarity might not breed content, but it does encourage short-sightedness and bias. Consequently, writing this has been like reading a map with familiar contours and boundaries, but which cannot be unfolded correctly. We try to impose later meanings on the original. In other words, as a historian, the task in hand here has been revisionary – seeing again what was once familiar.

What has been certain – and it acted as a compass – was that the geography of my childhood, in Churwell, Beeston, Oakwood and Halton, gave me a clear impression of those divisions every great city has. These are marked, in England, by class, wealth, immigration, sub-cultures and so on. In that respect, Leeds, being a multi-cultural city, had a richness in evidence when I was a child in the 1950s. I have vivid memories of long walks into town from Roundhay, all the way down North Street and past the dispensary, taking in the vibrant, exotic shops along the route – everything from Jewish and East European clothes and food to the clothing retailers, which of course were abundant in this city of tailors and seamstresses.

Leeds's modern history is largely spun with cloth. Along with engineering, clothing manufacture forms the very substance of Leeds's identity, and this figures in the following stories. And at the heart of that we have a Jewish culture and network of families, and this extended into so much more, just as German immigrants did in Bradford. Leeds United has origins partly in Jewish social clubs, and so many of the traditional Leeds businesses were created by Jewish families. In terms of the Great War, as will be seen, there was a sensitivity to the activities of the Jewish citizens of Leeds. Through modern eyes, this is shameful, but it was of its time.

As for the civilians – they were soon to realize that they would have to endure shortages and restrictions, on top of the sheer apprehension of the fact that the death of a loved one was highly likely, given the nature of the war, both on sea and land. More than these experiences, in a sense, was the sheer intensity of the demand for change and adjustment, such as women taking over male occupations, output from factories being ruled by seemingly impossible targets, and the psychological and emotional stresses of staying an individual and having some remnants of privacy in a world that was increasingly open to scrutiny. You joined and contributed, or you were likely to be stigmatized.

My book will add to that testimony, and I have added some slightly unusual elements to the Leeds story of 1914–1919. These are in the accounts of some of the war-resisters, and in the material on the left-wing talkers and writers who had a presence in Leeds, particularly in the year of Revolution in Russia and its effects – 1917.

One of the strangest paradoxes of the whole period was the nature of the arch-enemy, Wilhelm II's Germany, and its relationship with Britain. Their opposition stems from the odd contradiction that the two states had a rich cultural interchange. German music, in particular, enjoyed a high reputation in Britain, and the cities of the two nations had productive and enjoyable links for concerts and lectures. This topic will reoccur when we look at 1915.

The aim of the book is to give a mix of narratives: a weaving of the home front and the theatres of war into the chronicle of the wartime experience of the people of the city, whether they were making shells, sewing uniforms, fighting the Germans, or merely battling to survive and make some kind of contribution. But I do have one purposeful additional element: I wanted to include biographical material on personalities who may not have figured in similar works and whose lives deserve to be much better known, particularly in Yorkshire. I refer here to Dorothy Una Ratcliffe, Sir Berkeley Moynihan and G. Studdert Kennedy ('Woodbine Willie' in the war). I hope my book goes some way to putting these individuals back in the picture.

There is one range of material included here also that illustrates the diversity of the Great War's scope and contents, when the massive subject is scaled down to a matter of archives and chronicles – the side-effects and spin-offs into areas of life affected by the war. The war itself was the spine of the period's *metanarrative* – the great national and worldwide story. This central story includes people from India and Australasia; it has people in the Middle East and in Africa involved, and yet my task is to bring the focus up close to one Yorkshire city. That entails a distortion, so I have purposely included reminders of the large picture. After all, Leeds people, when recalling experience of both world wars, often tended to recall the significant details, and these were very often incidents relating to the wider world. My grandfather, for instance, mentioned earlier, only came to know London because he was called in to do bricklaying. In the Second World War, my father (a stoker on a minesweeper) saw the USA and actually had a drink with the actress and singer Yvonne de Carlo.

That same process of rethinking and reshuffling previous lines of thought brought something else sharply into awareness when researching these stories: the heroes and heroines who were there, quietly doing amazingly impressive things, and who came to light, looking at cameras, their faces showing the strain and endurance. This was encapsulated on one page of W.H. Scott's 1923 history of the war in Leeds. The page has portrait photos of three women: Lady Dorothy Wood, who was Commandant of Temple Newsam Voluntary Aid Detachment (VAD) Hospital; Miss E.S. Innes, Royal Red Cross (RRC), Matron-in-Chief, 2nd Northern General Hospital; and Miss E.M. Cliff, OBE, Commandant, Gledhow Hall VAD Hospital. My point is that they all share something that overrides and cancels out class, background and status – a quality of dedicated self-sacrifice. They *are* their roles. They *are* their duties. The pictures show that.

War might do unspeakably brutal things to people, but it does broaden the mind and reset the moral compass. Writing about wars tends to do the same, I have found. From the very beginning in the Leeds Pals story, for instance, the photographic and diary records bear witness to something deeper and richer than any war: the men grew in character, empathy and in sheer resilience. Despite all the terrible images of death and suffering in that mythic landscape of Northern France and Belgium, there is the sense that, as one reads the chronicle of that adventure, there was something grand and indefinable in the spirit beneath the uniforms and the drills.

Chapter One

1914: The Call to Arms

Some years become iconic in themselves, with no further explanation or details required. They erase anything else that may have happened under the rule of their few numbers, and they indicate merely one event: 1914 was such a year.

At the turn of the nineteenth century, the city of Leeds had become one of the major industrial sites in Britain, and was generating skills and products to feed the massive empire. Its primary expertise was in engineering, clothing manufacture, dyeing and tanning. As the Victorian years marched on, there had been a proliferation of satellite industries that were spawned by the main ones, such as coal mining, ironworks and transport. All this was on top of the agricultural base too, which comprised all the bordering agricultural areas, from Wakefield in the south to Collingham and Wetherby to the north.

At the heart of all this there had been population growth and a steady but marked increase in urban development. In fact, in the last years of the nineties, a report on 'Leeds Slumdom' painted a depressing picture of the intensely red-brick terraces that were crammed into Hunslet, Holbeck, Wortley and Beeston. The worst instances of unhealthy living for the workers in the burgeoning industries were in the cellars. The report noted, 'I cannot refrain from saying that cellar dwellings are the most abominable feature of the Judas-like greed for rent which disgraces some of the property owners of today.' The author adds that poor sanitation was a feature also: 'I observed that in one

Title page from D.B. Foster's study of Leeds poverty. *Leeds Slumdom, 1897*

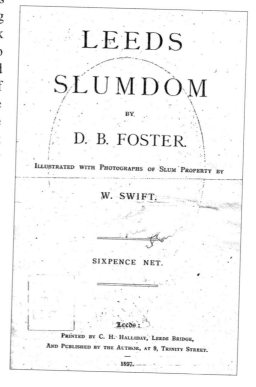

LEEDS

SLUMDOM

BY

D. B. FOSTER.

Illustrated with Photographs of Slum Property by

W. SWIFT.

SIXPENCE NET.

Leeds:

Printed by C. H. Halliday, Leeds Bridge,
And Published by the Author, at 9, Trinity Street.

1897.

district a very faulty arrangement exists in connection with the street drainage … the street drain is very much more used in crowded areas than in the better-class districts.' One of the worst examples illustrated that attempts to improve matters had caused even more problems: 'quantities of sediment' tended to 'give off bad smells' and the result was that sewer gas escaped out into the main open street.

Leeds only officially became a city in March 1893. It was not the first borough to be elevated to city status in Victoria's reign; Manchester was a city in 1853 and Liverpool in 1880. When Alderman John Ward chaired a special meeting of the city council that March, he held up a copy of the Royal Charter. It was a momentous occasion, confirming the fact that Leeds was a definite presence, with its own strong identity, near the end of that great imperial century.

Maps of the years just before 1914 confirm this urban growth. Beeston, for instance, in 1905, was at the end of the long tramway winding from Hunslet near the city centre, out up Beeston Hill and by Cross Flats Park. To the other side of this divide there were lines and lines of streets stretching widely across Beeston Hill and towards Middleton, where there was a colliery. Similarly, if we look at Holbeck and New Wortley in about 1890, we see a massive stretch of urban housing to the west of the London and North Western line railway. Then across to Holbeck, incorporating the Victoria iron foundry, Marshall's Mill and the engine sheds and repair works of the railway, there is even more housing.

Yet this is not to insist that Leeds was a desperately poor concentration of oppressed workers, with no cultural life and little diversity. That is not at all true. When war with Germany broke out in August 1914, the city had a thriving higher education base, theatres and music halls – entertainment in all quarters, from brass bands to park concerts. The Edwardians and Georgians loved to sing, dance and hold parades and concerts. At the drop of a hat, there would be something community-based going on. The families were strongly bonded in close-knit areas, and working-class life was intensely geared towards self-help and support.

Around the city there were the big houses: being a place for entrepreneurs, Leeds had generated wealth, and to the north of the city in particular there were the impressive villas and mansions of the masters of industry. Partly because of the Jewish immigration earlier in the nineteenth century and partly as a result of the rise of domestic industry and piecework, Leeds had become a booming centre of all aspects of clothing manufacture, and an element of this was retail: the central market was a thriving centre of trading (it was the place where Marks and Spencer began), and around the rim of the very heart of the city at Boar Lane, the Corn Exchange and at Leeds Bridge, the clothing firms were well established.

There had been widespread construction and reconstruction in the forty years before 1900. A publication of 1909 notes:

> The whole district on the east of Briggate has been enormously changed, largely through the construction of these markets as well as by the natural increase of the population. The Vicarage is gone. Vicar Lane has been widened … The fields through which the Sheepscar Beck found its way to the Aire are now covered with houses and factories.

In the years just before 1914, the city was also experiencing a degree of political turmoil. As Derek Fraser puts it, in his account of Leeds's political life at the time, 'The last months of 1913 had seen a big upsurge in Labour's electoral support – 50 per cent up on the poor results of the previous year and the beginning of a full-scale strike of the council's workpeople that was to end in defeat for the strikers one month later.' By 1916, as we shall see in my chapter for that year, the Labour presence was important in the overall debate about conscription and pacifism generally.

With all this in mind, it may easily be seen that when war was inevitable, Leeds was destined to be a principal source of every kind of constituent that might be needed for the war effort. Then the war came. On 5 August, England declared war on Germany, as that state had invaded Belgium and attacked France – allies of the British crown. The army and navy were mobilized and the Territorial forces were made ready to move into action. By the 15th of that month, Leeds men were already on their way to the theatre of war, as the Leeds Rifles left for the

The present building in City Square, formerly the Majestic cinema, also a recruiting office in 1914. *Author*

front, and within a month, casualties of the conflict were being brought home.

As so often happens in the story of events of great magnitude in history, there are apocryphal tales about the beginning. The Great War has plenty of these, as tragedy and drama are thinly divided from dark humour and farce. For instance, this is a supposed list of messages:

From Admiralty to destroyer flotilla at sea:
BRITISH ULTIMATUM TO GERMANY EXPIRES AT 23.00.

From Admiralty:
COMMENCE HOSTILITIES WITH GERMANY.

From flotilla leader:
IMPORTANCE OF WEARING CLEAN UNDER-CLOTHES IN ACTION IS STRESSED. THIS MAY MAKE ALL THE DIFFERENCE BETWEEN A CLEAN AND A SUPPURATING WOUND.

But of course, a war had been a possibility for a while, but when it came, the shock was very intense. From 28 June, when Archduke Franz Ferdinand was killed, and war for Britain on 4 August, there was a trajectory of feeling going from puzzlement to horror. Many had no real comprehension of the consequences of the assassination, including the Prime Minister, H.H. Asquith, who wrote to his beloved Venetia Stanley, 'we are in measurable, or imaginable, distance of a real Armageddon. Happily, there seems to be no reason why we should be anything more than spectators.'

The task before the people of Leeds was summarized by their mayor, Edward Brotherton, who later wrote, referring to the first months of the war, 'When war broke out, my activities as Lord Mayor were directed primarily to two things – the obtaining of recruits for the Forces and the continued provision of employment for the wage earners.' He wasted no time: he held a meeting in the Town Hall, gathering together the principal employers in the area. He put the problem simply but powerfully: 'What the future would bring forth was hidden from us, but in order to prevent distress … we all undertook to keep our factories going at least half-time.'

The effort to contribute to the determination to defeat the Kaiser's army was immediate and resolute. A special correspondent from *The Times* went north just ten days after the war began and he chose as his headline, 'The Grim Resolve of Yorkshire'. He reported that 'the spirit of the people is magnificent' and that adjustments were being made in industry:

> Many operatives are preparing to go on short commons for the sake of their mates who have been called to the colours. At many collieries the men who remain behind have voluntarily decided to pay 2d a week to help the families of the Territorials and reservists who have been called up for service from the pits. In some Leeds engineering works the men are performing the same service in a different way. Overtime is to be worked and the pay accruing from it is to go wholly to a fund for the upkeep of the homes of fellow employees who have joined the colours.

BUSINESS MEN
SHOW YOUR PATRIOTISM
Your Country Needs YOU
HER PERIL IS GREAT
JOIN THE
LEEDS CITY BATTALION
(Age Limit 19 to 35)
Register yourselves at the
TOWN HALL, LEEDS
Open Daily: 9 a.m. to 9 p.m.
Your friends are joining
WHY NOT YOU?
E. A. BROTHERTON, Lord Mayor.

An appeal to the suited types of Leeds to don khaki.

The Territorial forces had been rationalized by legislation a few years earlier. A look through the papers, such as the *Daily Graphic*, in the 1890s and early 1900s, gives a very clear impression of a militaristic race: there are detailed features on training, rifle contests, summer military manoeuvres, accounts of the fleet and the latest warships, and so on. It comes as no surprise to learn that when the British Expeditionary Force (BEF) was needed to move quickly to France in

August 1914 and fight the first engagements, the Regular Army needed the Territorial back-up. The fact is that Germany had hatched its Schlieffen Plan – the notion that two fronts could be created, towards France to the west, and facing Russia in the east, and that men could be moved swiftly by train from east to west, as Russia would take so long to move its vast armies across huge tracts of land.

The call for volunteers came after the shock of the first encounters in France, at which it was soon realized that many more infantry would be needed to man the long lines across the front, protecting Paris and also the sea coast. If the latter fell, the Germans would have the best ports for attacking Britain.

A typical recruitment poster.
Author's collection

Lord Kitchener, Secretary of State for War, appealed for the new armies. The urgency of the situation was stressed when people noted that at Mons, on 23 August, the British Expeditionary Force had their first real battle and had had to withdraw. By 9 September, Fred Wilson, of the Fifth Royal Irish Lancers, was back in Leeds, invalided, and he spoke to the press:

> He … says he has seen the Germans bayonet our wounded as they came across the field and forced women and children in front of them as they passed our guns. He reckons nothing of the fighting power of the Germans. 'They are,' he says, 'simply whining, howling cowards. They were fairly peppered in five charges, and when their cavalry saw us coming they whined like dogs.'

That brand of morale boosting was to become increasingly common as the war ground on.

Kitchener wanted 100,000 men, and the poster calling for volunteers explained, 'Lord Kitchener is confident that this appeal will be at once responded to by all those who have the safety of the empire at heart.' The age of enlistment was from nineteen to thirty and men signed up for three years, 'or until the war is concluded'.

The response for the Pals' battalions was astonishing. Throughout the war, Leeds was to have almost 90,000 men fighting in the services, and 9,640 were killed in action. As was the case throughout the land, men would sign up for a range of regiments, but the bulk of the volunteers joined up with the 'Pals' or the 'Bantams' battalions. There was also a demand for unmarried junior officers for temporary commissions. These places were soon taken up, and within a month there were announcements that the officer places had been filled.

There were other parades and enlistments as well as those of the new 'Kitchener' men. The volunteers and Territorials were also keen to be seen.

One report said that there was 'brisk recruiting':

> The Fenton Street barracks have been found too small to accommodate all the men and guns and a detachment has accordingly taken up quarters at the Headingley football ground. The 7th battalion of the West Yorkshire Regiment paraded at the Carlton Hill barracks at 9. They were dismissed to their homes before noon.

There was a meeting at the Town Hall in Leeds, to start the drive for recruitment; the Lord Mayor was totally involved. This was Edward

A page from *Chums* magazine. Note the influence on the new battalions – **Chums and Pals.** *Author's collection*

The Leeds Town Hall, where so much organization for war began.
Author's collection

Brotherton, who figured prominently in the work for the home front. The lines of recruits appeared, and there was no smoothly efficient method of processing them with any speed. The first recruiting office

A Leeds tram used for recruitment. Note the destination – Berlin!
Leeds Library

was at Hanover Square, and almost 2,000 men were ready to sign up. The Tramways Committee then helped by allowing the use of their office at Swinegate for recruitment. There was also another recruitment ploy – the use of a tram, lighted, and with the destination 'Berlin' on the front. Fred Wilson, already quoted regarding the lack of mettle of the enemy, went with the Mayor and Lady Mayoress on the tram. The lady in question was a considerable literary figure – Dorothy Una Ratcliffe; she had married Charles Ratcliffe, nephew of the Mayor, Edward Brotherton, in 1909, and she was very much involved in war work. Her biographer, F.E. Halliday, explained, 'During the war she helped regularly in hospital work. She assisted Edward Brotherton in his raising and equipping of the Leeds Pals … Lieutenant Victor Ratcliffe, her husband Charles's brother, was killed in action near Fricourt.'

The Leeds Pals were, properly, the 15th (Service) Battalion (1st Leeds) The Prince of Wales's Own (West Yorkshire Regiment). The basic rationale behind this initiative was that men would join up and then serve with their friends and workmates; it was the brainchild of Major General Henry Rawlinson, although it was Lord Derby who conferred with Kitchener about the idea. Of course, the battalions since then have always been linked to Kitchener and that powerful poster on which his austere face confronts the viewer, demanding attention.

Regarding the notion of 'chums' and 'pals' in this context, the main reference relates to the words in popular usage, and much of this was derived from the immensely popular boys' periodical, simply called *Chums*, in which there were roaring adventures and deeds of derring-do.

Raising a battalion meant that they had to be equipped. Photographs from all parts of Britain showing the new soldiers training make it clear that for some time, their uniforms and equipment were far from professional. But the process of turning the working men into soldiers was well documented in Leeds. A picture of the time shows a group of men being measured for their uniforms in September. The training ground at Colsterdale was settled on, and practical matters such as a water supply were undertaken. A photo of some recruits on board the light railway going to Colsterdale from Masham shows that all the men were still in 'civvies' and looking cheerful. The trajectory in front of them was firstly, months of basic training in England, then a transfer to another camp, and finally, transport over the Channel to the front.

There were also the workers' battalions: in this case, the Leeds Rifles. On 17 September, the press reported that 'About 950 men have given all their names for the two workers' battalions which are to form the reserve

An anonymous Tommy in a Pals' camp. *Author's collection*

of the 7th and 8th Leeds Rifles. It is understood that a Jewish contingent of at least 350 will join, bringing the total to date of 1,300.' The Jewish reference is interesting. *The Leeds Mercury* even thought it worthwhile to take a picture of a line of Jewish men waiting to enlist outside the Town Hall. In that age when anti-Semitism was still apparent in many quarters, there was still a persistent ideology that Jewish people have no allegiance to any homeland; that they are a transient concept when nationalism and patriotism rear their heads. It was also a time in which Zionism was being discussed and was a hot topic, and when the question of internment of aliens came to prominence, there were plenty of Jewish people around Leeds with, of course, German surnames.

Then there were the Bantams. On 18 January 1915, they took part in their first parade. The press reported:

> The Leeds 'Bantams' Battalion, in full khaki rig-out, held their first parade in strength through the streets of Leeds on Saturday. The whole of the route was densely lined with spectators, whose regard for 'the little men with the big hearts' was evinced by the cheering. The picture shows Major Pollard at the head of the battalion marching through City Square.

Bantams were men under the height of 5 feet 3 inches. As with the other recruits, the local papers took a great interest in their movements during the training period.

By early 1915 they were on the move, and later they were at Skipton and Ilkley, following the camps used by the Bradford Pals. After that it was Masham. They were the 17th Service Battalion of the Prince of Wales's Own West Yorkshire Regiment, and their place in the great theatre of war was explained in *The Yorkshire Post*: 'On the other side of the valley are several other camps, and the troops with whom the Bantams will be associated in field work include new units from Manchester, the Northumberland Fusiliers, the Lancashire Fusiliers, the Royal Scots … and the ever useful Army Service Corps.' The paper was keen to give a boost to the morale of

Recruitment poster for a Bantam battalion.

the Bantams, and included this praise: 'In spite of their lack of inches, the men look a very useful body, and with the higher military education and the better physical training they will get at Masham, it needs no prophet to predict that they will justify the highest hopes.'

The ranks of the officers were fed also by the men from the Officers' Training Corps in the universities. An anonymous correspondent from Leeds wrote to *The Times* to point out that the universities were not burying their heads in the sand and simply carrying on with their studies:

Sir,

Sir Cyprian Bridge mistakes the spirit of the universities at this crisis. There is no slackness or shirking. A closer knowledge of them, and of the Officers' Training Corps, would reassure him. Here ... the number of applicants for commissions in the army is already about one in five of the men students. The University Contingent of the OTC, depleted by men going on active service, is again full to overflowing. Besides this, the members of the university have provided forty skilled interpreters for work in military hospitals and a body of sixty-four men and 170 women have been trained here for service in voluntary aid detachments.

Of course, some potential soldiers were turned away. One report of such an occasion gives a useful explanation:

Some weeks ago three workmen from a large engineering works wished to join the Pals battalion which has been raised in Leeds. Scarcely had the applications been made when an urgent request came from the War Office that they should not be proceeded with, because at this juncture the men's services were of most value to their country in their regular calling.

It was to be a massive effort in every sense, supporting the swarms of men who were training for France, and those who were already there. Just a month after war was declared, there was a Flag Day, linked to a general appeal for help in gathering materials and comforts for the wounded soldiers. It was to be an appeal that lasted through the years of war, as familiar as the sound of marching men or the moans about shortages. The *Yorkshire Evening Post* ran a feature on this that shows the work of 'total war' mentality:

In due course an appeal will be made for comforts to sustain the soldiers during the coming winter campaign. In the meantime, lists of the little luxuries needed, supplied by the commanding officers of units at the front, show a remarkably curious diversity. Tobacco and cigarettes are, of course, the first essential, but other things asked for include pipes, letter pads with pencils, playing cards, dominoes, mouth organs, matches, shaving and other soaps, Vaseline, tin whistles, cakes, footballs, draughts ... Tonight no fewer than 4,500 boxes will be in the hands of the collectors ... A number of ladies have offered their services for collecting in the central thoroughfares ... Collections in the outer portions of the city will be taken by children.

The last months of 1914 brought all kinds of responses and initiatives, as well as the military recruitment. A centrally important event was the arrival of the Zeppelins, the airships that carried the war to the shores of England, dropping bombs on Scarborough, Whitby, Hartlepool and Cleethorpes. There were deaths in those attacks, and as *The Times* reported, this was the cause of 'a new rally to the colours'. The Zeppelins were the German airships. They were rigid airships, designed by Count Ferdinand von Zeppelin, and they first took to the air in 1900. One of the very early flights was witnessed by a writer, Stefan Zweig, and it ripped from its moorings and was whipped away – an inauspicious beginning for what would be a menace to Britain. Zweig wrote about the very first flight as well: 'I was on my way to Belgium and happened to be in Strasbourg where ... it circled the Munster ... That evening, news came that it had crashed in Echterdingen.'

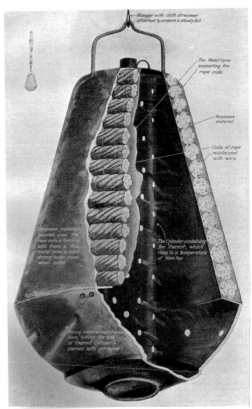

Leeds people knew the East Coast towns very well, and they associated them with summer holidays. This made the attacks all the more terrifying. There were heavy casualties: forty-four died and sixty-six were injured. The very thought of these giant balloon-like monsters floating above England and bringing death and destruction on what was now becoming 'the home front' was terrifying. They were very difficult to approach at that time: the height they flew at meant that planes could not intercept them, and also, they were out of the range of the ground-based anti-aircraft guns.

A drawing of a bomb, such as would have hit Scarborough.
The War in Europe, *1919.*

When such a horrendous thing happened, naturally there was an atmosphere of fear and panic, and also a flow of misinformation, scaremongering and apprehension. One rhyme that circulated then was:

Absolute evidence I have none –
But my aunt's charwoman's sister's son
Heard the policeman in Downing Street
Say to a housemaid on his beat
That he has a brother, who has a friend
Who knows the day when the war will end ...

One woman wrote in her diary: 'The raid night was horrid. I got E & S into a big building ... every moment we expected to hear the bombs drop close by or on us, for the machines sounded overhead.'

There had never before been attacks like this over the British mainland. The heart of the massive British Empire was under threat from an enemy who came by air, not by sea. That fact alone was shocking. Obviously, the Yorkshire towns that had been hit were not so far from Leeds: it all seemed too fearsome to contemplate. One press report was: 'At Scarborough three churches, hotels and many private houses were wrecked or damaged. Seventeen people were killed. At Whitby, sad to relate, the ruins of the famous old abbey were still further laid low. Two people were killed and two wounded.'

If anyone thinking about the Zeppelin attacks, with hindsight, wanted to claim that their regime was only a minor part of the war, let them make a note of Max Wall's account of a Zeppelin hitting his childhood home:

Before being destroyed, the Zeppelin had discharged an aerial torpedo and a gas bomb, and both of them arrived at the same point: our home in Baytree Road, Brixton. My elder brother Alec and I, who were sleeping together on a large iron bedstead, were buried under the rubble of the demolished house, our lives saved by being trapped under the bed ... I can still hear the sound of the rescuers digging and clearing away the rubble, and I can remember how we could see chinks of daylight between various cracks in the brickwork while both of us were yelling for someone to save us.

The need for medical provision – both for treatment and for convalescence – became obvious by the last months of the year. The local papers carried extensive hospital lists, such as one from January 1915 that lists casualties from the British Expeditionary Force who were in the 2nd Northern General Hospital (Beckett Park) in Leeds. There was to be a massive and enthusiastic effort from all quarters to cater for these wounded men. One interesting glimpse is a photo, in *The Leeds Mercury*, of a theatrical company called Venus Ltd visiting sick men at Beckett Park. The caption reads, 'The members of Venus Ltd Company, who are appearing at the Leeds Empire this week, entertained the wounded soldiers. The picture shows Miss Jennie Benson, the principal, handing cigarettes to the patients.' Jennie, one press report said, enjoyed a high reputation as a 'character actress, singer and comedienne'. It was valuable work, and the Benson Company, run by impresario Sir Frank Benson, was to put on shows at the Garrison Theatre at Ripon Camp. In 1914, *The Stage Year Book* reminded readers that 'The occupants of military hospitals throughout the land have been cheered and helped enormously by the services, ungrudgingly given, of music hall artistes. They have helped the wounded heroes to forget for a brief spell their tragic experiences and their pain.'

There was also a desperate need for chaplains in the hospitals, too. Clearly, there was death stalking the wards. Treatment was all very well, but when the patient died, there was spiritual comfort needed also. In Leeds there was a team for chaplaincy provision, and we know something of the work through the memoirs of Lieutenant Colonel J.F. Phillips, based at the 2nd Northern General Hospital. He wrote about the worst, most demanding element in his duties:

> It was not long after the declaration of war before heavily laden trains were bearing the wounded and sick to various parts of the kingdom. Speedy as was the transformation at Beckett Park, there was no marking time before the first convoy arrived from the battlefields of France. They came with the soil of France upon their greatcoats, a few with support walked from the ambulance to the wards, the rest the stretcher bearers carried, some were entirely covered from view and of these some would not have been recognized by those who knew them best. That first arrival sent a thrill through Leeds and it was not least felt by the officers, nurses and ward orderlies at the hospitals.

Images of wounded fighters were becoming increasingly common by the last months of the year. In September, Beckett Park hospital had taken its first patients after the Battle of the Marne; the place had been transformed from being the City of Leeds Training College to a major military hospital. In the heart of the city, behind the Town Hall, was the Leeds Infirmary, which had been designed by George Gilbert Scott, and opened in 1868. In the year before the war, the King Edward Memorial

look on this page
and think of me
when far away
Perhaps I ee he

         E. A. Keel

            Coldstream Guards.

An autograph from a patient at a military hospital. *Author's collection*

Wing had been opened. But there was far more extensive provision for the casualties of the war as the months wore on: hospitals all around the city opened, and only 20 miles to the north there was Harrogate, which was celebrated for its convalescent and special water treatment facilities, along with other similar locations such as Ilkley. Places large and small were to be used, as the numbers of the wounded grew apace, and every hospital or home had its story. Arthington House, for instance, or the Ida Hospital, was more generally known as the Cookridge Convalescent Hospital, and had been founded back in 1886 when John North gave £6,000 to create a convalescent home in memory of his daughter, Ida. As was the case with so many such places, it was requisitioned in the war.

The war and its medical demands were to bring to prominence a number of outstanding medical professionals. Many nurses answered the call, working with several organizations, from the Red Cross to the Queen Alexandra's Imperial Military Nursing Service (QAIMNS). Quakers and other non-combatants manned the Field Ambulance Units, and as a broad basis for all kinds of help and support in the theatre of war there was the YMCA, of which more later.

Berkeley Moynihan, who was to become Lord Berkeley Moynihan with stacks of letters after his name, is without doubt one of the heroes of Leeds who is barely known to people of the city. He was born in Malta and his family had long-standing military connections; his father had won the Victoria Cross at the siege of the Redan in the Crimean War, killing five Russians in hand-to-hand fighting, and later served with distinction in the Indian Mutiny. Naturally, young Berkeley went to Sandhurst, but it was not for him: he was cut out to be a doctor, and he started his studies at the Leeds School of Medicine in 1883, graduating in 1887.

Moynihan was the most successful British surgeon of the Edwardian period, specializing in surgery of the stomach, gall bladder and intestines. At the time when he was learning his profession, the whole abdomen was rarely explored surgically; that was only done in extreme emergencies and almost always ended in the death of the patient. But there was more to Moynihan than his medical specialism. He was prominent in the Great War and in later life became a public figure of great authority, speaking before the most respected and high-ranking people in society. He was a sociable, charismatic figure. In his obituary, it was said:

> Moynihan was wholly incapable of holding a subordinate position. He was a born leader, and he enjoyed the fame, both professional and public, for which he had not long to wait. It became usual for surgeons from all parts of the world to visit Leeds General Infirmary to watch his method.

In the years just after he qualified, Moynihan did many things, as a person early in a career tends to do: he was self-supporting and made a little money from his private practice but he had to be freelance and work with what we call today 'a wide portfolio'. This extended to assisting the top surgeon, Mr Jessop, and working as the prison surgeon for Leeds, looking after healthcare in the prison. But this also involved a duty he hated: he had to be present at every execution in Armley. However, as his biographer Donald Bateman has said, there were deep satisfactions, even early on:

> Lastly, he was paid for the work he did as one of the official teachers of anatomy in the Yorkshire College, to which position he was raised in 1894. That work gave him great pleasure; he had always had a natural flair for anatomy, and early recognized the supreme importance of its detailed knowledge to the surgeon.

Moynihan's first cases included a wound below an eye, gout, and spinal tuberculosis amongst others. His very first operation was the drainage of a suppurating gland in the groin. The whole treatment involved eleven visits and plenty of dressings, and it cost the patient thirty-five pounds and eleven shillings.

In 1893 he passed the examination to become a Master of Surgery and was house surgeon at Leeds. Then he became Professor of Clinical Surgery in 1909. He was knighted in 1912.

Moynihan travelled across the world to learn more about his chosen profession from the experts in their fields: although he was a learned and dedicated man, his attitude towards his patients and peers was always sensitive and open-minded. The Hippocratic credo that 'the patient comes first' always counted for something with him. He was so impressive and successful that his

Leeds Infirmary – a key location in the care of the wounded. *Author's collection*

fame spread far beyond Leeds. He became the first provincial surgeon to be elected to the Royal College of Surgeons. He came to realize that England was not keeping up with developments in surgery elsewhere and also that there was no sharing of information with surgeons and hospitals overseas. Communication in this context had countless benefits for all concerned, and Moynihan's remedy was to found a journal that would act as a focal point for knowledge and research: the *British Journal of Surgery*. This allowed a group of surgeons to associate together, as a kind of club. Moynihan was in his element; he had been involved with clubs and professional gatherings all his life.

When the Great War came along in 1914, Moynihan was the ideal person to hold a senior position in the army, and was made the main consultant surgeon to the Northern Command. With a rank of major general, he served on the Western Front and with the British Expeditionary Force. This was at a time when medical work in the army concentrated on the body rather than the mind, so illnesses related to neurasthenia and battle stress would have been marginal concerns for him; he mended limbs and entered the abdomen to work on organs. Faced with a massive number of casualties each day, he worked under pressure and found it extremely stressful. This kind of experience invariably has its positives, and surgeons learnt a great deal from the many and diverse cases they had to deal with during the war.

W.H. Scott makes a special point, in his history of Leeds in the war, of highlighting the humanity and dedication of Moynihan, recounting him telling this story:

> The thing which struck me most was the patient heroism and uncomplaining fortitude of men after being severely wounded. The single instance I chiefly recall was connected with a boy H..., who had been badly smashed around the knee joint. He lost a great deal of blood; his wounds were septic by the time he reached hospital. We tried to save his limb and his life, but gas gangrene set in, and we had to amputate the thigh and the hip joint.
>
> He was a miracle of stoic endurance and cheeriness. After the amputation it was clear he would die, for the gangrene spread on to the abdomen. When I went on my tucking-up round at midnight he was far gone. I leaned over and said, 'Well old boy, how are you?' He raised his white face till his chin was over the bedclothes and husked out, 'Tip-top, Sir, tip-top.' He was dead in less than half an hour.

In a letter to *The Times* in 1923 Moynihan makes it clear that he was the foremost representative of his profession at the time, writing about the definition and standing of surgery. In the course of that letter he explained the element in the work that is not often expressed: 'The practice of clinical surgery makes a further heavy demand upon qualities of temperament and of character which are little exercised in the cloistered tranquillity of the laboratory.' That was one side of his work well explained; the other was the issue of what general practising surgeons were achieving in comparison with the 'scientific' achievements of researchers: 'But there are physicians and surgeons whose lives have been spent in the wards and in the operation theatres of our hospitals whose contributions to "scientific" medicine are entitled to rank with this [academic work].'

In other words, in later life Moynihan had taken on the role of public educator, distinguished speaker and spokesman. If the press wanted an opinion or a comment on a topical medical issue, they went to Berkeley Moynihan. In addition to the speaking and expression of opinions, Moynihan wrote a medical best-seller: *Abdominal Operations*. It was typical of the man to have done that, as he was a meticulous writer in everyday practice, leaving detailed notes on cases from the very beginning.

Berkeley Moynihan became Baron Moynihan of Leeds in 1929.

Leeds gave him the honorary freedom of the city and the university made him Vice Chancellor in the Jubilee Year of 1924. Honours constantly came his way and he reached the status of a well-known public figure. Few men attain that place in which their portrait is painted and hung at 'Headquarters' of a profession, but Moynihan did – his portrait being painted by Richard Jack, RA, and presented to the Royal College of Surgeons. His number of honorary degrees was fourteen: maybe a record.

Lord Berkeley Moynihan died aged seventy-one on 7 September 1936 at his home at Carr Manor, Meanwood, in Leeds. His son, Patrick, became a barrister, no doubt inheriting some of Moynihan's charisma and dedication to his career.

In October 1914, there was an additional problem for the home front: the plight of the Belgian refugees. Many of these casualties of war had arrived in England with practically nothing, having had to leave their possessions back home. Dame Flora Lugard, an author and journalist, supervised the War Refugee Committee and the wheels of charity swung into motion. There was a widespread appeal for help, as accommodation for these people was sorely needed. On 13 October, the press announced that 6,000 Belgians had landed in Folkestone from Ostend, and that in fact almost 100,000 refugees had arrived here by the end of October. In a survey of the areas that had taken these unfortunates, Leeds was mentioned:

> One can understand the difficulty of finding even temporary shelter for refugees at the rate of some thousands a day, but as Lord Gladstone stated yesterday, 'Somehow it has been done.' The work of the War Refugee Committee has been simplified in one or two cases, by the action of some localities … Leeds has taken 1,000. If other districts would follow this admirable example the pressure on the headquarters would be greatly relieved.

In Leeds, Helen Briggs was the treasurer of the committee, and her note to her peers explaining the provisions established was placed in *The Yorkshire Post*. Her words were, 'We house at the present time [November 1914] 1,200 refugees in Leeds, and owing to the magnificent response to the appeal made through the press, furnished houses in all parts of the city have been placed at the disposal of the committee.' The first destination for the Belgians was the Town Hall, and although the initial intention was to retain a family together in one house, soon this had to be changed to allow for more families to be placed together in what was available. For instance, as researchers at Project Inspire (a group who recently produced a summary of the war effort) have established, Morley Hall was used to house Belgians, as confirmed on the Leeds website Leodis (see the bibliography).

Helen Briggs explained also that the refugees were given a living allowance, and all donations for this went through a system for payment based at the Town Hall. From the fund, the men received five shillings and the women four shillings. On top of this, clothing was provided, having been taken to a number of food depots. By 12 November, *The Yorkshire Post* noted, with the sad fact of there being a number of families still without the essential help, that, 'friends will gladly contribute to meet the increasing necessities of our Belgian visitors.'

A typical example of the kindness and generosity of the people of Leeds is that of the Pontefract Lane Quaker Adult School. They wrote a letter to the Belgian Vice Consul, and the gist of this, as *The Yorkshire Post* reported, was that they were 'stating their readiness to give hospitality to thirty Belgian women and children on the school premises'.

One particular refugee we know a lot about is René Lefèvre, because the Lady Mayoress at the time wrote about him. Dorothy Una Ratcliffe was involved in the efforts to help the Belgians, and she recalled meeting René. She saw him at the Central Station, after the fall of Antwerp, and she had been brought in because she spoke French fluently. Dorothy recalled seeing the lost wanderers arrive in a crowd:

> Amongst them was René Lefèvre … he came up quietly and apologized for troubling me. He was about twenty-seven years of age, tall, and very thin. His clothes were much too light for our Yorkshire climate. His smoke-grey eyes looked very tired; his skin was sallow, his hair was thick, fair and wavy. When he spoke his lips trembled … He used his hands expressively and I noticed that though travel-soiled, they were delicately shaped.

The writer Dorothy U. Ratcliffe, who worked with refugees.
D.U.R. A Memoir, Wilfrid J. Halliday

He was a violinist and he had lost his instrument. He waited for other trains and searched everywhere, and Dorothy helped him, but with no luck. He was being housed in Roundhay, and he was alone – with no family anywhere. After a long settling-in period, he eventually earned money and opened up a little. Finally, Dorothy gave him her own violin. The story reads like an object lesson in charity and caring, as René was destined to stand in for another violinist and play with a professional outfit – the Leeds Symphony Orchestra.

Everything was certainly not rosy, though, regarding the refugees; there are always those in any community who will complain, and some voices were raised, suggesting that many of these Belgians should go back across the Channel and fight alongside our men. *The Leeds Mercury* responded with a feature proclaiming, 'The Belgians in Leeds – none left who are eligible for King Albert's army', and the details were given:

> In view of recent complaints that among the Belgian refugees in Leeds are some who ought to be serving in their own army, it is interesting to learn from the Committee that there is not left in the city a single Belgian who is eligible for military service. ... Moreover, it is satisfactory to hear that all the males, with only about twenty-five exceptions, are working and earning something which goes towards maintenance of their families.

Dorothy, the Lady Mayoress, was indeed one of the markedly successful movers and shakers of Leeds in the first year of the war. She formed a committee, the Leeds Lady Mayoress's Committee, and it was described admirably by W.H. Scott in his history of Leeds in the war years:

> Starting operations in temporary rooms at the Town Hall, and removing first to offices in East Parade and then to Basinghall Buildings, a general committee of sixty ladies, with an executive of half that number, were finally installed in commodious premises at No. 4 Park Row. Here, with a devoted and untiring energy worthy of the highest praise, they

Albion Court – a scene of busy and dedicated administration in support of travelling servicemen. *Author's collection*

adhered to their self-imposed task until the victory of the Allied armies made it possible for them to close their many activities in the early summer of 1919.

What the succession of lady mayoresses did at first was set about having clothes made for the wounded men who would go to Beckett Park. Their practical achievements provide a very long list, but a few of the most notable were wheelchairs for the hospitals, motor ambulances, 174,000 bandages, and much more. They even had a 'Music in Wartime' committee, and the relish for fun and entertainment went on unabated.

There was one particular talent that Leeds folk had well established by the time of war – raising funds. Towns and cities across the land were asked to raise funds for war relief, armaments, producing tanks, and acquiring medical supplies (even to the extent of gathering sphagnum moss to be used for dressings). One reason for this was poverty: the sickness arising from the lifestyles of the urban workers, and the centrality of the workhouse for those who fell out of the labour force, meant that funding was large scale. One way to see this is to look at the report of the Bramley District Nursing Association for the year ending March 1914. This existed to provide professionally trained nurses for the sick poor at no cost. Grants and funds that year came from such sources as performances of the Bramley Band and the Leeds Workpeople's Hospital Fund. The total raised was £89. That should be multiplied by forty to arrive at something like the modern value. Nothing was wasted and the smallest gifts were gratefully received: Mrs Ross of Brown's Terrace had donated some child crutches, and Mrs Simons of Bath Avenue donated old linen and a bed-bath.

The mindset of domestic economy and charity eventing was well rooted in when the call came for war funds.

There was also, of course, a commodity in high demand that Leeds was significantly able to supply – clothing. The Northern Area Clothing Depot was set up in the tram sheds in Swinegate. This was to be the place where over 50 million shirts and 30 million pairs of boots, along with trousers, socks and anything else required by the Tommies, were made. Such a large-scale operation was bound to have teething troubles.

On 21 August, the Leeds Committee of the Amalgamated Union of Clothing Operatives were not happy about some arrangements being made. The *Yorkshire Evening Post* explained the problem: the union were unhappy about 'voluntary work by private ladies'. They wanted all the garments to be made by girls who were currently unemployed. There was certainly some unfairness going on, as Mr H.E. Whitley,

An iconic image of Leeds's tailoring industry.
Author's collection

Secretary of the Clothiers' Operatives Union, explained: 'Some of this work … has been done in the mills by women who are on short time, without any payment. They ought to be paid because there is no scarcity of money, and these women only get four pence an hour.'

There was no shortage of orders. On 21 August one report pointed out a massive order for army boots, and these details were given by Fred Wardle:

> A large trade is going to have a roaring time. A quantity of leather is manufactured in Leeds for army purposes, both for boots and accoutrements, and this is in very great demand just now. Upper leathers for army boots are all made in Leeds. … I believe that practically every branch of the leather trade will be busy.

Along with this, there was also the demand for clothing for the wounded, and everybody who could do so contributed to that effort. One newspaper showed a picture of four women at work, with the caption, 'Sewing parties busily engaged in making clothing for the wounded are to be seen all over the country. Our picture shows a party of girls hard at work in a lady's garden in Fenton Place, Leeds.'

What about the war itself? By the last months of 1914, after having forty-eight battalions in the field in August, losses had been heavy. In late August there had been the Battle of Mons, in which the British Expeditionary Force was pitted against the Germans, and the British came off well, but then, in early September, came the Marne. Some of the German forces had been transferred to the east, and the new thinking of their high command was to divert from the straight route to Paris. The army, led by Von Kluck, moved that way and inadvertently left a gap that was quickly exploited by the British. The ensuing struggle brought heavy losses. The focus of the Allies' thinking was to save Paris, and it was at this time that the taxis of the city were commandeered to shift men sharply to the front.

There followed the Battle of the Aisne, lasting until the end of September, and the first Battle of Ypres in November. In the first confrontation, the Germans had retired to the river Aisne, but they regrouped before the British could maximize their advantage. After that retreat and then the stand by the Germans, on higher ground, the future iconic feature of the war began in earnest – digging in and establishing trench systems.

As the narrative known as the Race to the Sea intensified, Ypres was to be the scene of desperate fighting and high casualty rates. The race was to protect the sea ports, maintaining the British hold on the bulkhead

A love letter home from the front, from W. Payne to his family in Horsforth. *Author's collection*

into the war zone. It was at Boulogne, for instance, that a huge military base was rooted in, with a large-scale transport hub in the heart of the entrenchments. The war was from the start controlled by railway routes: from the transport lines behind the theatre of war a shuttle service operated, taking troops to and from the front lines. They also serviced training camps behind the lines, such as the one Siegfried Sassoon was sent to – for rest and ordeals like refresher courses in bayonet training.

The fighting was at times desperate and determined. Press reports from the front were often highly dramatic, such as this from Compiegne:

> We could hear the crack of the rifles and see the German horses impaled on the bayonets of the front rank of the Guardsmen. Then the whole force of infantry and cavalry were mixed up in one confused heap. … Shells from the British and German batteries kept dropping close to the tangled mass of fighting men.

Chapter Two

1915: The War Escalates
All Fronts Severely Tested

The year began with a military tragedy – but not on the battlefields of France. It was much nearer to home, at Gainsborough, on the river Trent. In the village of Morton, a little north of the town, men of the 3rd West Riding Territorial Brigade were there for training in the construction and use of pontoons, but matters went badly wrong. The result was a heroic tale, involving, amongst others, a Leeds solicitor, Lance Corporal Arthur Chorley.

In the previous October, 4,000 Yorkshiremen had gone to Gainsborough for training and they stayed with the local families. On 19 February, men from D Company started raft building in a gyme (a pond, local dialect) at Morton. There is no accurate statistic as to how many men were on a particular raft when it keeled over, but one estimate is forty. The raft went over, and men were plunged into the water. Their comrades were watching from the bank and many dived in to try to save lives. One man, George Sykes, wrote an account later in which he said that he threw off his coat and his pack, then 'dived into the water and tried to save the poor chaps. It was awful! We could not tell who was drowning or who was wanting help, and we got two out just in time.' Chorley and Lance Corporal Chappelle saved several men, and Walter Gatenby returned repeatedly to save men, up to the point that he was too tired to carry on. Chorley's actions were outstanding, as he dived in a number of times to save others in the pool.

After a roll call, it was discovered that seven men had died. It took a long and determined search to look for more bodies, but two men – Howgate and Hough – kept this work up for some considerable time. The corpses were laid out at the nearby Crooked Billet public house, and this was followed by an inquest held at Morton School. The dead men's families began to arrive, and the bodies were moved to the Holy Trinity Institute Hall before being taken to their homes in Dewsbury, Batley and elsewhere.

IN SORROWFUL REMEMBRANCE

OF

Seven British Soldiers,

**Privates W. DENT, E. COCKILL, J. MYERS,
F. COOKE, A. BRUCE, E. BATTY,
W. ATHERON,**

"D" Co., 4th Battalion, K.O.Y.L.I.,

*Who were accidentally drowned in the Gymes, Morton,
Gainsborough, while doing their duty,*

ON FRIDAY, FEBRUARY 19th, 1915

A memorial card from the Morton tragedy. *Author's collection*

Obviously, in such cases there is the subject of blame as soon as the reasons for the disaster are identified. The officer in charge at the time was Captain Harold Hirst. At the inquest, the opinion was expressed that the raft had been far too small to carry a large number of men. Also, local knowledge dictated that the gymes were very deep, and careful preparations would have seen the sense of using the shallow lake at Thonock Park instead.

Captain Hirst was to meet his death in June that year and he is buried at Bois Grenier; the hero of the incident, Chorley, became a captain later, but then he was one of the thousands who died at the Somme. The dead

A contemporary postcard of the village of Morton. *Author's collection*

soldiers were: Private W. Dent of Leeds; K. Cockill, W. Atheson and V. Cooke of Wakefield; J. Myers of Dewsbury; M. Batty of Batley; and A. Bruce of Harrogate.

To Leeds folk, that February must have been black and dismal indeed: as well as the horrors of those drowning, there was a railway accident just outside the new station in the city. As one report put it, the train 'had only proceeded 250 yards when a rear coach failed to take one of the numerous sets of points.' The driver managed to pull up the train just a few yards short of a bridge, otherwise, as the report continues, 'three coaches … would have been thrown over the bridge into a yard 50 feet below.' There were 160 passengers on those coaches.

In this year everybody was training for mobilization, from the proper soldiers down to a vast array of ancillary workers and participants. For instance, the West Riding RASC Motor Transport Volunteers, 'with a strength of twenty and a small committee', was gathering. The abbreviation is Royal Army Service Corps, and the ASC generally was rather uncharitably known by the old sweats as 'Ally Sloper's Cavalry', after the cartoon character. But this group were serious about their work. Scott describes their assembly as they formed under Alderman Charles H. Wilson, who had been gazetted out of the Prince of Wales's Own West Yorkshire Regiment:

> He was invited to take command of the Leeds group on 12 October 1915, and it soon grew into a useful and powerful unit. Under various names and various formations, nearly 700 men were enrolled. Of these, 150 passed into Regular units, several obtaining commissions, and many becoming non-commissioned officers.

The officers, not to be outdone by the New Army, went to camp, going to Burton Agnes and Ripley Valley. As usual with such secondary outfits, as W.H. Scott notes, it was not 'formally recognized by the War Office, and, no special duties being allotted to it, the OC was told to "carry on" and find such work as could usefully be done.'

There was also industrial trouble. From early January to the second week of February, a miners' strike looked likely: 50,000 members of the Yorkshire Miners' Association held a strike ballot on 12 January, after there had been a decision by a conciliation board to advise new pay percentages. A two-thirds majority was needed, but the press were sure that arbitration would settle the affair. The root cause of the problem was the Minimum Wage Act, which should have led to a rise of 5 per cent in three stages, but the union representatives insisted that the men had received nothing of that. The mine owners ordered a few pence a day

Leeds Pals unloading at Colsterdale, 1914. *Leeds Library*

to be paid, but no new percentages. The Miners' Federation supported the Yorkshire men and it seemed as though the affair would drag on.

It did. But in the first days of February, the correspondent from *The Times* wrote that government intervention was imminent, and added, 'Tonight I learn that before this is likely to happen an effort will be made by the parties to the dispute to bring about an amicable settlement.' The owners agreed to pay no less than 15 per cent of two-thirds of the minimum wage. All was resolved, but then there was more labour trouble.

The clothing trade was now in ferment. In January there had been plenty of celebration of the industry, with reports noting how important and successful Leeds was in producing 'the khaki':

The government have recognized the importance of the city as the natural distributing centre for the West Riding by making it the seat of a new Army Clothing Depot to relieve the congestion at Pimlico. A new tramway shed in Swinegate has been taken over from the Corporation, and it [is] being fitted up as a khaki exchange. The floor of the spacious structure is almost covered by immense rolls of strong army cloth, fresh from the mills, and waiting to be made up into overcoats and uniforms. The depot could not be more happily situated, for the clothing factories of Leeds are almost as important of its many-sided industry as its woollen mills.

Then, in early February, came the threat of a strike. The root cause of the discontent was unequal pay. The larger firms with more modern machinery were paying a higher rate than the small companies, and every available outfit was busy producing the khaki. A first meeting of union and employers led to an enquiry and a tour of the firms not paying the higher rate. A conciliation board was involved and they insisted that they had to be consulted before any mass sackings, which had been threatened by some.

A mass meeting of the workers was held on the evening of 9 February with regard to possibly calling a strike. Of course, as there was a war on, the army knew about the trouble and they insisted on being told about the grievances. Unfortunately, the employers said that they had no real information about the problems and couldn't supply details to the military representatives. This led to an impasse and a resolution of the issues, but the signs were there for more powerful and organized unions to emerge in the clothing industry in the future; it was a Leeds woman, Anne Loughlin, who was one of the leaders and innovators. She was born in 1894, the daughter of a shoemaker of Irish descent. Anne was just sixteen when her father died, and she started work for threepence an hour in a clothing factory. By 1915, she was an organizer for the National Union of Tailor and Garment Workers, and in the following year she was in control of a major strike in Hebden Bridge.

This all came as a shock, considering how bright and optimistic things were towards the end of 1914 for the clothing industry. The Wholesale Clothiers' Association had announced how pleased they were that they were expecting government orders, and they told the press: 'Members be recommended as far as possible not to dismiss any operative, and that efforts should be made to work at least half-time, the work to be divided equally in each grade.'

The Morton tragedy had been merely one incident in the midst of a massive logistical exercise of moving the Pals' battalions and other forces to the training camps. The Northern Command of the army was using Colsterdale and Ripon, as well as other smaller camps, and the men of the Leeds Pals, along with other battalions containing Leeds men, were adjusting to camp life early in the year. Laurie Milner, who has written an exhaustive account of the Leeds Pals, has provided detailed material on the life, regulations and activities at the Ripon camps. The printed regulations give a very clear idea of the regime, and these items dealt with every conceivable aspect of communal life there. Many of the instructions were schoolmasterly, such as, 'On Field Days care must be taken not to break down fences or leave gates open.' The tone was often that of a school trip, and indeed a sense of adventure and elation may be observed in the copious photographs preserved at the Leeds Library and in the archives of *The Yorkshire Post*, amongst other places.

Memoirs from the ranks of the new recruits as well as from the seasoned professionals who knew Ripon, are many and varied. There can be few sharper contrasts in the history of the camps than that at Studley Royal, from how it was described in mid-Victorian times to how it was when transformed for military habitation. In 1875, A.C. Price, the author of a history of the area, wrote:

> After passing through the village of Studley, and arriving at the park lodge, the eye is restrained from excursion into the woodlands by a noble avenue of limes, above a mile in length, that guides our path and directs the eye to the church … the eye, that will be gladdened by nothing but nature, naked and unadorned, now appears joyfully through the thicket on an irregular pool.

Pals at dinner time, Ripon Camp. *Author's collection*

Some Tommies learning to dig trenches. *Author's collection*

In comparison, we have this account from Private Tony Miller, a soldier in the Leeds Pals: 'I joined the signallers because I thought I'd get out of drilling and guard duty, and I did. Instead of doing a lot of guard duty we were learning the signals. … We used to have rolls of wire to hug around and we used to have Morse code flags.' He also adds a touch of dark humour: 'We used to have sacks hung between posts and we used to charge these sacks and jab 'em with a bayonet … I thought if I were to miss these particular sacks in the charge and stab somebody, it'd be awkward.'

Naturally, organization was not always impressive, as another Leeds recruit commented in his notebook:

At last, we reached camp. The huts were all that could be desired, but something had gone wrong with the commissary department and there was not a thing for us to eat when we arrived. Many of the fellows broke camp and made their way to a nearby village and to inns. About three hours later, those who stayed hopefully and faithfully in camp received an issue of tea, bread and jam.

He also summed up the training: 'Forming fours, route marching, applying bandages, physical jerks, polishing buttons and kit inspections etc.'

Kitchener had approved the plans for a camp at Ripon, with the aim of having one working by April. There was to be accommodation for over 30,000 men. The problem was that such a massive establishment would generate local difficulties of all kinds. This was explained in a meeting in London in March to create a string of girls' patriotic clubs across the land. Lady Frances Balfour gave a speech, followed by one from Emily Kinnard, who put her finger on the problem. She referred to 'a great enthusiasm for khaki', expanding on this with these words, as reported in *The Times*:

> A great number of troops would be drafted into places where formerly there were not enough men to go round, and the girls would see the prospect of nice engagements resulting, or else, as in Ripon, where 14,000 troops had been drafted into a town of 8,000 people, the soldiers would crowd the population uncomfortably and have no place for the young girls to go of an evening.

The reasoning behind the planning of training camps of such massive size was that it made sense for a division, which was a block of fighting men within a battle order and a campaign and which needed to train as well as fight together. Three infantry brigades constituted a division, and each brigade had four battalions, so the new army fitted in with the overall structure – with men coming from various locations to meet and work with the other constituents of their division. In practical terms, as the camps were made across the country, the huts had to be made to take about 800,000 troops. In Northern Command, there were 200,000 men. As early as just a few weeks into the war, the Directorate of Fortifications and Works set about issuing orders, along with specifications, for the new huts, which were named after Major Armstrong, who commanded the Directorate. Armstrong's hut was to be 60 feet long, 20 feet wide and 10 feet high. Each hut would hold thirty men. On top of this, there were other designated buildings such as sites for cooking, resources and supplies, a guardroom and so on. Fir timber was used for the construction, and also corrugated iron. Fortunately for those inside, asbestos was sampled and tested, but then rejected.

The extent of the camps was indeed impressive. Ripon camps held about 15,000 men. In some places reservoirs had to be made, and power sources installed. There is no doubt that the logistics of planning and making the camps provide evidence of skilful and intelligent construction work. The army got some things right. The railway back-up continued through the war, with, for instance, a line from Littlethorpe to one of the camps. Later, from October 1917, an ambulance train for wounded men was shown to the public in Bower Road yard, and as David Thornton, a historian of Leeds, has noted, 'Despite the very bad weather the train attracted 2,551 visitors who paid, to the Red Cross, £145 0s 6d in admission charges.' Special exhibitions raised money very successfully, as Rogers adds, 'The previous April an egg and poultry demonstration train had attracted 1,360 people to Harrogate Station.'

The locals were not happy. All those men thrown together, with a heady mix of camaraderie and a sense of adventure, was a recipe for chaos. The main element contributing to the chaos was, as usual, drink. Pub visits were banned until six in the evening, and of course there was always the YMCA. The authorities hoped that smiling faces and soft drinks would be a substitute for the wilder aspects of free time. In addition, there was a view that hard work would subdue the spirits and bring more sleep and rest; the diaries of some of the soldiers there do paint a picture of an uneasy mix of physical jerks and free time. For instance, in David Raw's book on the Bradford Pals, he quotes Herbert Taylor's diary, and we have entries such as these:

19. Physical drill 6.45. Easy morning. Canteen corporal at 12 Company left at 3.00.
20. Did nothing all day. Company returned at 3.30. Lecture by Captain Davis.
21. Musketry all morning and afternoon.
22. Brigade route march over 18 miles by Brimham Rocks.

The basic regime of the camps, as conceived by the War Office, was to have bayonet and shooting training, recreation, consultation with medical staff, and gymnasium exercises, with a fundamental progression of esprit de corps and inculcation of the right military mindset, rooted in discipline and teamwork. Camps generally were not exactly liked and celebrated. Herbert Read, in the Green Howards, wrote in his diary:

I came to this dreadful place a week ago. The Medical Board gave me light duty – but they don't understand the term here … all the time the same monotonous work – shouting oneself hoarse, trying to initiate remarkably dense recruits into the mysteries of 'forming

The Leeds Battalion.

The Prince of Wales's Own West Yorkshire Regiment.

ORDERS FOR CAMP

BY

Lieut.-Colonel J. WALTER STEAD, V.D.

Town Hall, Leeds, *September 21st*, 1914.

1. CAMP.

The Battalion will encamp at Colsterdale on **Friday, September 25th, 1914.**

2. ADVANCE PARTY.

Men who have given in their names will attend at Headquarters, on **Tuesday, September 22nd**, between 6 p.m. and 8 p.m., to draw kitbags. It is recommended that those who can do so should bring in a pair of Blankets in a paper parcel for their own use. These will have a label attached with name and number and will be issued on arrival at Camp. Each man will receive a card showing the Company to which he has been posted, and on presenting this to the Quartermaster-Sergeant will receive his kitbag, to which the card will be affixed.

The advance party, under Sergeant-Major Yates, will parade with overcoats, sticks and kitbags, at the North Eastern Railway Station, Leeds, on **Wednesday, September 23rd**, 7.30 a.m.. and proceed by train to Masham for Colsterdale Camp.

3. ISSUE OF KITBAGS.

The remainder of the Battalion will attend at Headquarters, on **Wednesday, September 23rd**, between 4 p.m. and 8 p.m., to draw kitbags Owing to the scarcity of Camp equipment, it is recommended that those who can do so should then bring a pair of Blankets in paper parcel for own use. These will have a label attached with name and regimental number, and will be issued on arrival at Camp. Each man will receive a card showing the Company to which he has been posted, and will receive from the Quartermaster-Sergeant his kitbag with the card affixed.

4. ARTICLES TO BE BROUGHT.

Men will attend in plain clothes. with caps. sticks and overcoats, and each man is recommended to be in possession of the following articles in his kitbag :—Two pairs of socks, one shirt, pair of pants, hair brush and comb, tooth brush, clothes brush. small dubbin brush, razor and shaving brush, two towels, pair of strong leather laces, pair of shoes (canvas preferred) to wear in camp after drill. No unauthorized bags or boxes will be taken to Camp. Hair should be cut short.

5. OFFICERS' BAGGAGE.

Officers should arrange to have their baggage ready packed and labelled at Headquarters, not later than 8 p.m.. on **September 24th.**

6. BATTALION PARADE, SEPTEMBER 25th.

The Battalion will parade in plain clothes. with overcoats, sticks and kitbags, at the North Eastern Railway Station, Leeds, on **Friday, September 25th.** Men will fall in by Companies on the platform at 8.30 a.m., and afterwards proceed by rail to Masham for Colsterdale. On arrival at Masham kitbags will be collected and transported to the Camp.

7. ENTRAINING.

When entraining silence must be maintained as far as possible by all ranks to ensure expedition in the work. Men must not entrain until ordered.

8. HOURS OF REVEILLE, &c.

The Buglers will sound the following calls at the hours stated :—

Reveille	5.45 a.m.
Dress for parade	6.15 a.m.
Parade	6 30 a.m.
Retreat	7.0 p.m.
Tattoo, First Post	9.0 p.m.
Tattoo. Last Post	9.30 p.m.
Lights Out	9.45 p.m.

Absolute silence is to be maintained in Camp between the hours of Lights Out and Reveille.

9. SATURDAY'S PARADE,

The Battalion will parade as strong as possible on **September 26th**. at 6.30 a.m., for check roll-call All N.C.O.'s and Men, no matter how employed, must attend this parade. Employed men will be allowed to go back to their work when permission has been obtained. Pay Sergeants will attend with their pay-lists to check the names.

fours' etc. I think I shall flee to the front for a little peace at the earliest opportunity.

In spite of criticisms that may be levelled at the regimes in the camps, the fact is that they achieved the main purpose of solid training for war; even more than this, they had another, tougher, objective in some ways – to create the camaraderie so essential to the teamwork that may mean the difference between success and defeat in the theatre of war.

Of course, there was still a determined media assault on men to enlist. In the summer of this year, after a lull in recruiting, there was more interest, and it seems that the army had fastened on to the efficacy of having women, rather than tough sergeants, involved in encouraging men to take the King's shilling. The *Yorkshire Evening Post* reported that there was 'brisker enrolment than earlier in the week':

> Recruiting in Leeds yesterday was brisker than on previous days, and of the forty-five men who were attested fifteen were secured by the lady recruiters. The Royal Field Artillery, the Royal Army Medical Corps and the Royal Garrison Artillery have commenced recruiting again and yesterday nine men enlisted in Hanover Square. … Eighteen recruits were attested for the third line of the Leeds Rifles and ten men enlisted in the Cameron Highlanders (Territorials).

The press loved to regale their reports with photos of men being energetic for their country, though the pictures were not always indicative of proper soldiering. One double page has a good image of men doing rifle drill, but opposite this is a scene in which five men are wringing out cleaning cloths into buckets while two NCOs look on. But the documentary interest the reporters took was often chatty and upbeat, of course, as in this glimpse of a visit to Templenewsam Hall by the 3rd Battalion Leeds Volunteer Training Corps: 'The busy weekend concluded with an instructive field day in the park at Templenewsam. … Some little time after luncheon was spent in fraternising with the wounded soldiers in residence at the Hall, for whose benefit a collection was made.' As the war moves on, the reader may see that the press reporters become increasingly aware that the public want good news, and that any negative subjects (such as the slow recruiting figures) are played down. Their only hurdle in this enterprise was that group pictures of soldiers invariably look glum and dour, as if the poor infantry were only too aware that they were supposed to be cheerful at the thought of another round of duty with the mud and rats.

Men from the RAMC in camp at Salisbury Plain. *Author's collection*

It was a time of all kinds of emergency measures. Of course, there was the important matter of home security, and the police and fire services, together with volunteer older servicemen, were responsible for a number of matters. In Leeds, at the time of the war, the Fire Service was run by the police (as it had been in the City of London until c.1900); there had been the Zeppelin raids and there were fears of more, so fire and rescue had to be considered. In October 1910, the Police Weekly Rest Day Act was passed and the officers had to have a day off in every seven. Consequently, the special constables had to step in. On 6 August 1915, the Leeds public would have seen what looked like a response to a terrible fire. *The Yorkshire Post* tells the story:

> The explanation was that the newly formed amateur fire brigade, which will be available for service should the Zeppelins unhappily visit the city, were off for an afternoon's drill, their destination being the Headingley cricket ground. ... Chosen from the ranks of the special constables, these amateur firemen have spared no pains to make themselves efficient and the brigade a really useful body.
>
> They have made great sacrifices. ... Already the brigade has

been mobilized twice, and so complete is the organization that within half an hour practically all of the members of the force have been assembled at the Fire Station in Park Street, ready for service in whatever part of the city they might have been required.

A minimum squad was on duty every night between 10.00 pm and 2.00 am, and these were being trained on the job, going to actual fires with the regular force. The man in charge was Superintendent Tose, and he had his men put on a weekend drill for the press. The reporter told the Leeds folk, 'Of the eighty members there were sixty-seven on parade, and the absentees were mostly men who had been granted leave. ... In another week or two the brigade will be inspected by the Chief Constable.'

In the spring, there was an event that had a profound impact on the already entrenched panic and xenophobia that had bedevilled the land after the war began. With hindsight, it is strange to see, very clearly, that the closeness of Britain and Germany, in cultural aspects in particular, was always apparent. Of course, our Royal Family were partly of German descent, and when war began, Kaiser Wilhelm was supposed to have said, 'To think that George and Nicky [King George V and Nicholas, Tsar of Russia] should have played me false! If my grandmother (Victoria) had been alive, she would never have allowed it.'

The event in question was the sinking of the *Lusitania*. The outrage after this was savage and irrational: civilians on board had perished, after the vessel was torpedoed by a German U-boat. Gangs around Liverpool beat up anyone who might be considered to be German, so that included anyone with an un-English and vaguely European name. Properties with German-sounding names were prime targets. In Leeds and Bradford,

A close-up of the German U-boat that sank the *Lusitania*.
The Great War in Europe, *1919*

however, places with significant German and Jewish populations (in which names sounding Germanic would have made people vulnerable), there was little open trouble. Some of the irrational fear and hatred had the most terrible effects, such as explained in a letter to *The Times* in 2015, from Michael Myer, who wrote, 'My grandfather was not German. He was a Lithuanian Jew, but it did him no good trying to tell his neighbours that as they smashed up his shop. His name happened to be Schneiderman.'

A Czech gentleman wrote, anonymously, to *The Spectator* in April 1915, explaining something at the very heart of this paranoia about foreigners. He wrote, 'An invisible, yet for all that quite tangible, barrier seems to have arisen around me. I shriek from meeting you lest I be taken for a spy.' His point was that he had felt English, and been accepted as English, until the wartime fears spread the irrational behaviour he could see around him.

The issue of men in the ranks who came from German families was not so rare in Yorkshire: after all, there had been large waves of German immigrants throughout the nineteenth century to Bradford, Leeds and many other Yorkshire towns. The usual strategy was to adopt an English name, as was the case with the Steinthal brothers. Paul Steinthal joined the Royal Artillery as a Major Paul Petrie, and his brother Francis also took the name of Petrie.

There was nothing new in that xenophobia either. In her autobiography, mill girl Maggie Newbury recalled, referring to autumn 1914, 'We were soon to see some of the uglier aspects of war, when gangs of hooligans went and broke windows of shops owned by Germans. These shopkeepers were in the main good honest people who had served us well with their pork shops and delicatessens.'

Soon after war began, there was trouble. In Keighley, there were several attacks on shops owned by Germans just a few weeks after 4 August. Much of the focus for these attacks was on German butchers. Keir Waddington, a historian with a special interest in the use of sausages in German antipathy, notes that these butchers and their wares were 'a visible symbol of Germany and German influences on Britain'.

All this was evident in Leeds with the affair of Professor Schüddekopf, an academic at Leeds University, which highlights the nature of the xenophobia. In the violent atmosphere of the anti-German feeling in 1915, Schüddekopf, whose son had enlisted in the Leeds Rifles, made a discreet request to the high command that his son be sent anywhere except the Western Front, as he would be potentially facing his

An anti-German cartoon from 1890. Fun *magazine*

own relatives in battle. The news of this led to a campaign to sack Schüddekopf, as historian Frank Finlay explained in his account of the story: 'The Home Secretary explained that it implied nothing to his discredit and compassionately endorsed the suggestion that he withdraw on an extended leave of absence to the spa town of Harrogate, which promised respite and the distractions of a renowned musical scene.' It was a move to shift the source of embarrassment, but nevertheless, the subject reached Parliament.

Hansard reported the question and response regarding the Home Secretary's words on the affair. The issue was one of whether or not Schüddekopf would be interned. Hansard reported:

> Mr Butcher asked the Home Secretary whether his attention has been called to the case of Professor A.W. Schüddekopf of Leeds University, a German believed to be naturalized, whose son formerly held a commission as a second lieutenant in the Service Battalion in the 7th Leeds Rifles; whether ... Schüddekopf informed the commanding officer that he (the Professor) was a German ... and that he refused to allow his son to fight against Germans; whether Second Lieutenant Schüddekopf acquiesced in his father's views ... and has since resigned his commission ... whether Professor Schüddekopf still owes allegiance to the German Emperor, and whether ... he will order them to be interned?

The Home Secretary replied that Schüddekopf junior was now withdrawn from active service in the Rifles and was engaged in home defence work. He insisted that the Schüddekopfs had no allegiance to Kaiser Wilhelm. There were other quibbles, but a wider debate was opened up, and in that we learn some interesting facts. For instance, that from January to May of that year, 1,289 aliens were released from internment camps. But the anti-German paranoia was not going to go away easily. Sir Alfred Markham asked the Home Secretary how many aliens were still at liberty. He was told that there were 1,289 such people.

The Schüddekopf affair had put Leeds at the centre of the xenophobia.

At the mid-point of the year, shortages and economy were the watchwords on the home front. A typical feature in the press was 'Economy for Housekeepers' and the advice included a full weekly dietary, preceded by this very superior wording: 'It is only by "managing" as the poor people term it, that you can cater well for your family at present prices. I append a few days' suggested meals for a small family with two or three maids.' The wealthier middle and upper classes were no doubt also fretting about having the right kind of maids, never mind the dietary. But for the well-heeled, a typical day's food was: 'Tuesday. Breakfast, savoury rice; lunch, casserole of fish, potatoes, milk pudding; dinner, white soup, mutton cutlets with puree of onion and potato, stewed fruit and junket.' If evidence was needed that there were 'two Englands', then this should be compared with the general working-class Leeds day's eating, which was, according to my own family history (Hunslet), jam, bread and margarine with tea for most weekday meals, supplemented by whatever was being grown in the garden at the time.

The shortages were largely the result of a naval blockade in the North Sea. At the beginning of 1915 it had become clear that the war was on a far grander and almost incomprehensible scale than anyone had imagined when it began. What was also clear was that it would now be an effort involving everyone – men, women and children. Everyone had a part to play. Women, in particular, would be called upon to engage in all kinds of industrial work. Across the land, there were already a large number of trades that were carried out in small premises as family businesses, and women were involved in this, as is shown by the amazingly productive soldering and metal trade in Birmingham, for instance, where 'Grandma Page's factory' – a shed behind a house – was the place where a huge number of badges were made. The Great War certainly created a massive demand for such things. One woman when interviewed on the trade said, 'They made all the military badges.'

That involvement of women in war-based production was to become a major element in Leeds's war work, and as W.H. Scott wrote in 1923, 'Men everywhere were being released from industry and women were taking their places on the tramways and railways, in offices and workshops …' Those same women, on the home front, had to make do and mend, and use all available local resources.

Shortages and hard work apart, enjoyment still had to be found, and in 1915 that meant, more often than not, a night at the theatre – especially at the Varieties. Leeds City Varieties, the entrance nestling off Briggate and easy to pass by, began as a 'singing room' as part of the White Swan public house, which had opened for business in June 1865. Thornton, the arcades man, owned it, but he sold it in 1876, by auction. It was leased to John Stansfield and then passed to his daughter. In 1894 the place acquired

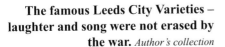

The famous Leeds City Varieties – laughter and song were not erased by the war. *Author's collection*

The comedian Wilkie Baird, who played at the Hippodrome, Leeds, two weeks before war broke out.
Author's collection

the name City Varieties, and it later became known to millions well beyond Leeds when television cameras filmed the show *The Good Old Days* from there from 1953–83.

It's possible to trace the story back even further, because in 1760, when the White Swan was built, the 'singing room' clearly witnessed all sorts of 'turns' from customers of all kinds and abilities. In 1908, the Ordnance Survey map shows the area it covered, and we know that it had a balcony, and that it had a capacity to house an audience of 2,000. There was even a snooker room somewhere within its walls.

In 1880, Stansfield put his name to the concern, letting it be known as Stansfield's Varieties. It became part of a larger outfit when Charles Morritt took over in 1880, as he owned other similar properties. But by 1894, it was Leeds City Varieties Music Hall to the locals.

In 1898, the Empire Theatre was constructed just along the road in Briggate, and so the Varieties was sold. But the new owner wanted to maintain the music hall tradition and it was reopened in 1898, run by J.C. Whiteman.

Music halls were booming in the 'Naughty Nineties' and personalities who trod the boards in Leeds in that decade included Charlie Chaplin, Lillie Langtry, the Jersey Belle, and even Harry Houdini, who was about to experience his failure with the Tetley challenge (see Chapter 16). It was a time when there was a deep interest in regional identity and 'difference', so dialect performers in songs, comic monologues and sketches were popular. An example was the 'Eight Lancashire Lads' – one of whom was Chaplin. But there was also the Lancashire comedian, Morny Cash.

Fred Wood had been in charge, and he had also run the Queen's Theatre in Holbeck, but he died in 1913. The main opposition to success

THE KAISER'S DREAM.

THERE'S a story now current, though strange it
      may seem,
    Of the great Kaiser Bill and a wonderful dream.
    Being tired of the Allies, he lay down in bed,
And, amongst other things he dreamt he was dead.
On leaving the earth to Heaven, he went straight,
Arriving up there, he knocked at the gate,
But St. Peter looked out, and in voice loud and clear,
Said " Begone Kaiser Bill, we don't want you here."
Well, says the Kaiser, that's very uncivil,
I suppose after that, I must go to the Devil ?
So he turned on his heel, and off he did go
At the top of his speed to the regions below,
And when he got there he was filled with dismay,
For, while waiting outside, he heard Old Nick say
To his imps : " Now look here, boys, I give you all warning,
I'm expecting the Kaiser down here in the morning ;
But don't let him in, for to me its quite clear,
He's a very bad man, and we don't want him here.
If he ever gets in we'll have no end of quarrels,
In fact, I'm afraid he'll corrupt our good morals."
" Oh, Satan, my dear friend," the Kaiser then cried,
" Excuse me for listening while waiting outside ;
If you don't admit me, then where can I go,
Oh do let me in, for I'm feeling quite cold.
And if you want money, I've plenty of gold ;
Let me sit in a corner, no matter how hot ; "
" No, no," said Old Nickie, " most certainly not ;
We do not admit folks for riches or wealth ;
Here are sulphur and matches, make a Hell for yourself."
Then he kicked William out, and vanished in smoke,
And just at that moment the Kaiser awoke.
He jumped out of bed in a shivering sweat ;
And said " Well, that dream I'll never forget ;
That I won't go to Heaven I know very well,
But it's really too bad to be kicked out of Hell."

A postcard with a poem to the Kaiser. *Author's collection* at that time was the coming of the silent films. Across the country, a number of music halls were so much in the middle of hard times that they were demolished, but not so the Varieties: it struggled on, though not perhaps with the usual class of performing stars. But it really was the age of variety, even to the extent of acts being 'novelty' – a term that covered a variety of sins as well as stars. Certainly that trend is exemplified by the work of Bryant and Bryant, billed as 'Australia's Novelty Manipulators'. They were the Edwardian equivalent of David Copperfield or similar today.

Of course, there was always another dimension to variety and that was entirely local. This was a tradition that carried on well into the twentieth century, as in the 'turns' put on every week at working men's clubs, when local talent had its turn. In 1913, the Varieties gave locals a chance to entertain by holding amateur wrestling matches – something that accessed the 'gala' or company sports day trend.

Biographer Stephen Griffin has described the acts in the great age of variety in the Edwardian years:

> Some of the variety acts were downright bizarre: along with the usual tumblers, acrobats, fire eaters, jugglers, ventriloquists, dog acts, contortionists and conjurers there was, for instance, a man who appeared on stage dressed in a voluminous coat, within which was contained virtually any train ticket or card that anyone could name; his whole act was based on audience members calling out the most obscure journey they could imagine.

The stories of many singers and performers who were destined to make it either in the world of variety, theatre or operetta are often extraordinary, such as that of Lilian Neilson, of whom an early biography said:

> The story of Lilian Neilson's life is largely a story of hardship and sorrow. She was born out of wedlock, in or near Leeds, March 3 (probably) 1846. Her father's name is unknown, her mother, an actress, was Miss Brown. She was reared in humble circumstances and worked in a factory.

But the theatre stories are often charming 'rags to riches' ones, and Neilson somehow 'obtained a footing in the theatre and little by little she made her way to a position of some influence.' Her first big break was playing Juliet at Margate. So many of the Varieties people had comparable lives.

In the war period, any kind of appeal was tried. In 1915, for instance, not only was there a challenge to Leeds men to come to the theatre and take up a debut as a wrestler, but there were exotic, crazy shows such as the aforementioned Bryant and Bryant's Australian Novelties.

On 30 April the news finally came in the national press of the fate of Leeds prisoner of war Private William Lonsdale, who had been a tram conductor. There was a great deal of uncertainty as to his fate, and *The Times* reported that he had been sentenced to two to ten years' imprisonment for striking a German officer:

> The assault for which Lonsdale was committed was on Nov 9. A number of British prisoners on that day, because of sickness, declined to go to work, but were driven out of their tent with rifle butts. Lonsdale struck his Landwehr Guard on the chest with his fist, whereupon a non-commissioned officer intervened and struck him with his sword. On 31 December Lonsdale was sentenced to death by a Superior Military Court, to which the court of the court martial had appealed. Lonsdale then applied to the Imperial Military Court through his legal adviser for a revision of his sentence.

Varying reports were then received: some said he has now sentenced to twenty years inside, and others that he was to die. The truth appears to be that he was eventually repatriated on 2 January 1919, and he sent a telegram home, writing, 'Arrived at Edinburgh, 4 o'clock. Arrived safe, Leith. Another wire later. Bill.' Apparently he had written home earlier, saying, 'I have left everything to him [his lawyer]. The men who have to attend to my wants treat me with civility and respect.'

The heavy fighting over in France and Flanders brought news of numerous acts of extreme heroism, and some Leeds men figured in the awards. Among these were some recipients of the Victoria Cross. This is the highest military award for conspicuous gallantry, and was created in 1856 during the period of the Crimean War. It was, from the beginning, open to all ranks. The cross has a crimson ribbon with the words 'For Valour' written on it. The very first crosses were made from Russian guns captured at the battle of Sebastopol.

A publication of 1893 describes the scene in Hyde Park when Queen Victoria presented the first crosses:

> Sixty-two men of valour received the Victoria Cross from Her Majesty in Hyde Park on the 26th of June. Multitudes flocked to see the interesting distribution. The Victoria Cross is a very plain

affair, made out of the cannon captured at Sebastopol; a little leaden coloured Maltese cross with a red ribbon for the army and a blue ribbon for the navy. The decoration carries with it a pension of £10 per annum. The Queen, with that air of majesty and condescension so natural to her, pinned the cross on each brave breast.

John Raynes, though born in Sheffield, died in Leeds and his body lies in Harehills Cemetery. He won his VC in France in 1915 and the explanation is given in *The London Gazette* on 18 November, that year. He was in A Battery, Royal Field Artillery, 71st Brigade. The citation notes that his battery was under heavy bombardment and the shells coming down on them were armour-piercing ones. There was a cry of ceasefire and Raynes went out to help the wounded. Sergeant Ayres was wounded and several hundred yards away from comparative safety when Raynes got to him and bandaged him. The casualty was then carried to a dugout and then Raynes went out again.

Later that day, having already been gassed because he had given his mask to a wounded man, Raynes was in a group of men, some of whom were buried in a house, and others in the cellar beneath. Although he was wounded he stayed behind to help others. The citation concludes: 'Then, after having his wounds dressed, he reported himself immediately for duty with his battery, which was again heavily shelled.'

Raynes had joined the army on 10 October 1904, becoming a reserve bombardier and so was recalled to the colours when war broke out. When he came home he joined Leeds City Police, and it comes as no surprise to learn that this astonishingly able and brave man won promotion to sergeant. He retired from that profession in 1926 because of spinal injuries he had sustained, and died in 1929 after being paralyzed for three years. Just before he died, he received a telegram from other Yorkshire VC winners. He died two days after the Lord Mayor of Leeds, N.G. Morrison, had visited him.

Another soldier to have been awarded the VC was Company Sergeant Major Harry Daniels, who had been part of a force that advanced into no-man's-land, facing the usual terrain of open land and barbed wire. Daniels, with Corporal Noble, rushed to cut wires, and they were wounded. Harry Daniels lived until 1953. He is buried at Lawnswood. Although not originally from Leeds, he lived in the city on his return from the war.

Neuve Chappelle was another scene of a hard scrap. This battle, in March 1915, generated some outstanding military experience, as one would expect, bearing in mind that British casualties in that action numbered about 11,600. Sir John French wanted Neuve Chapelle taken, and the Germans did what they usually did – brought a sustained mass of shellfire to 'flatten out' opposition. But the Allies got in first this time. The first British assault was against the arm of the enemy commanded by Crown Prince Rupprecht of Bavaria, and an account written not long afterwards describes what happened:

> Hell opened its mouth and belched forth fire and brimstone. The wind was torn, the ear pierced by the rush and roar of high explosives and shrapnel shells. A wall of fire fell upon the German trenches, and the men in them were dazed. … Many went mad with horror … the hail of shell continued, the gunners working with a grim joy as they marked how, under the bombardment from their huge Howitzers firing lyddite, the enemy's trenches fell in. … Meantime, the troops who were to make the charge waited.

These were the men of five brigades of the 8th Division. They dashed at the German trenches, and mostly this was a smooth operation. But one man from the 23rd Brigade found that wires in front were uncut, and they were vulnerable when trying to get through. Later, when the advance was resumed, things went wrong. Then, after 12 March, the Germans brought in considerable reinforcements. Nevertheless, counter-attacks proved effective and the result was advantageous to the Allies. This is an action backed up by staggering facts: the British losses included 190 officers and 2,337 men, with over 8,000 wounded as well.

Sir John French, Commander-in-Chief of the British Armies in France and Flanders, sent an Order of the Day message to Sir Douglas Haig and the 1st Army:

> I am anxious to express to you my warmest appreciation of the skilful manner in which you have carried out your orders, and my fervent and most heartfelt appreciation of the magnificent gallantry and devoted, tenacious courage displayed by all ranks whom you have ably led to success.

This engagement, in the context of family history, has an instance of the difficulties in locating records of the fallen. For most researchers, the result of enquiry is to find – as is the case with John Blackburn from Leeds, for instance – that a date of death is all that may be found. But at Neuve Chapelle, as we know from enquiries undertaken by Lieutenant Colonel Stevenson of the Royal Engineers, we have an interesting subject. Stevenson was finding out where his grandfather, Private Patrick Ruddy, of the 2nd Battalion, Yorkshire Regiment, was commemorated.

He had no luck in the search, but then, with some documents to help, the date of death was found. But there was no record. The solution seems to be that a 'Thomas' Ruddy's death was recorded, and the dates tally. It was a clerical error, it appears. All this is important because in a war with so many deaths and so little proper occasion for burial and record keeping, ancestors disappear and the full story is lost. Neuve Chapelle was that kind of confrontation.

The Leeds Rifles had a hard time of it in 1915, too. The reports of deaths filtered relentlessly into the local papers, and a typical instance is that of Lieutenant Richard Briggs. We have a brief but exact report:

> The 1st-7th Battalion West Yorkshire Regiment (Leeds Rifles) have sustained another sad loss by the death of Lieu Richard Stanley Briggs, the only son of Mr and Mrs F.D. Briggs of Pytchley House, Chapel Allerton, Leeds. Lieu Briggs was only twenty years of age, and he joined the Leeds Rifles two years ago. He went to the front with his regiment in April. When he met his death he was in his dugout, and a shell landed right on top of it, killing him instantly. He was a popular young officer, of great promise and his loss will be keenly felt. He was educated at Charterhouse and Emmanuel College, Cambridge.

The Leeds Rifles had already seen action in some of the worst places on the Western Front, and they were to go on to win the Croix de Guerre at Bligny Ridge, as will be described later. By the end of 1915 they were, as the *Yorkshire Evening Post* reported, 'to have a well-earned rest', in the words of General Sir Herbert Plumer of the 4th West Riding Division, who 'has a special interest in Leeds'. The report goes on to describe the Rifles' year:

> True, they have not been engaged in any big engagement, but they have nevertheless been in a hot corner the whole of the time. Their casualties have been by no means slight. Indeed, it would give the folks at home an unpleasant surprise if they knew the total number of men killed and wounded in both battalions.

What was their rest? The answer is that they were moved well back, out of the range of fire of any kind. The reporter notes that they will be able to play football there.

With reference to sport, it has to be recalled that the professional footballers, cricketers and rugby players had mostly joined the colours as well, and in the summer of 1915, one of these stars was killed. The war had of course been taking place at sea and in the air, as well as in

¡GHT

DECEMBER 25, 1914.

The Royal Aero Club of the United Kingdom
▪🏵▪ OFFICIAL NOTICES TO MEMBERS 🏵▪

THE FLYING SERVICES FUND.

and Administered by the Royal Aero Club for the Benefit Royal Naval Air Service and the Royal Flying Corps.

e ago Mr. André Michelin, Chairman of the Michelin Tyre oached the Royal Aero Club, with regard to a suggestion de to the Admiralty and War Office, that a general fund hed,

roceeds of which would be distributed at the end of the to all British aviators (or their dependents) having nplished deeds of daring."

ichelin offered to open the fund with a contribution of and asked The Club to undertake the organisation and ation of the Fund.

rds Commissioners of the Admiralty and the Army Council, preciating Mr. Michelin's generosity, did not think it to establish such a fund, but the following suggestions e :—

the Lords Commissioners of the Admiralty—

General Fund for the benefit of the Royal Naval Air ice to supplement the provision for officers, and especially , of the Air Service who are permanently prevented by nds or injuries, received on duty, from contributing to their support ; and for the wives and dependents of those killed tion.

the Army Council—

General Fund for the benefit of the Royal Flying Corps to evoted to the provision of pensions for military aviators nanently incapacitated, and for the families of such as are d ; but it is suggested that the rank and file should be the to benefit.

ichelin concurred with these suggestions and confirmed his ubscribe £1,000.

ords Commissioners of the Admiralty and the Army Council d of the Fund being administered by the Royal Aero Club, Club then agreed to organise and administer the Fund.

SPECIAL GENERAL MEETING.

ssor A. K. Huntington presided at the Special General held on Monday last, the 21st inst.

question as to the advisability of the Club subscribing the £1,000 to the Flying Services Fund was discussed, and t the speakers were the following members :—Professor A. ntington, Mr. Ernest C. Bucknall (Hon. Treasurer), Mr. Brewer, Mr. Martin Dale, Lieut. N. Pemberton Billing, R., Mr. John Cates, Flight Lieut. F. K. McClean, R.N.A.S., G. Grey, Mr. C. G. Grunhold, Capt. R. K. Bagnall-Wild, and Mr. C. F. Pollock.

Griffith Brewer moved :—

That the Club contribute £1,000 to the Flying Services Fund."

was seconded by Flight Lieut. F. K. McClean, R.N.A.S., rried, the voting being 20 in favour and 11 against.

y Members attended the Meeting.

SPECIAL COMMITTEE MEETING.

pecial Meeting of the Committee was held on Monday, the st., when there were present : Prof. A. K. Huntington, in hair, Mr. Griffith Brewer, Mr. Ernest C. Bucknall, Flight F. K. McClean, R.N.A.S., Mr. Alec Ogilvie, Mr. C. F. k, and the Assistant Secretary.

ction of Members.—The following New Members were d :—

Flight Lieut. John Marten Rush Cripps, R.N.A.S.
Ernest Edward Hooper.
Flight Lieut. Hugh Alexander Littleton, R.N.A.S.

iators' Certificates.—The granting of the following Aviators' cates was confirmed :—

987 Flight Sub-Lieut. Guy William Price, R.N.A.S. (Grahame-White Biplane, Grahame - White School, Hendon). Dec. 9th, 1914.

988 Flight Sub-Lieut. Bernard Osbourne Ffield, R.N.A.S. (Grahame-White Biplane, Grahame-White School, Hendon). Dec. 10th, 1914.

989 John Claude Horsey Barfield (L. and P. Biplane, London and Provincial School, Hendon). Dec. 12th, 1914.

990 Charles Percival Wilson (Maurice Farman Biplane, Military School, Brooklands). Dec. 14th, 1914.

The following Aviators' Certificates were granted :—

991 Flight Sub-Lieut. Thomas Spencer, R.N.A.S. (Maurice Farman Biplane, Netheravon Flying School, Netheravon). Oct. 27th, 1914.

992 Flight Sub-Lieut. Edward John Cooper, R.N.A.S. (Grahame-White Biplane, Grahame-White School, Hendon). Dec. 14th, 1914.

993 Flight Sub-Lieut. Percy Ethelwyn Hunt Wakeley, R.N.A.S. (Grahame - White Biplane, Grahame - White School, Hendon). Dec. 14th, 1914.

994 2nd Lieut. Malcolm David Methven (Maurice Farman Biplane, Netheravon Flying School, Netheravon). Dec. 14th, 1914.

995 2nd Lieut. Henry Bayly Reginald Grey-Edwards, R.F.A. (Maurice Farman Biplane, Military School, Brooklands). Dec. 14th, 1914.

996 George Gilbert Algernon Williams (Maurice Farman Biplane, Netheravon Flying School, Netheravon). Dec. 15th, 1914.

997 Stanley Graham Gilmour (Maurice Farman Biplane, Netheravon Flying School, Netheravon). Dec. 15th, 1914.

998 Lieut. James Cecil Thornton. R.F.A. (Maurice Farman Biplane, Netheravon Flying School, Netheravon). Dec. 15th, 1914.

999 Flight Lieut. Robert Hilton Jones, R.N.A.S. (Short Biplane, Royal Naval Flying School, Eastchurch). Dec. 17th, 1914.

1000 Flight Sub.-Lieut. Roger Martin Field, R.N.A.S. (Grahame-White Biplane, Grahame - White School, Hendon). Dec. 18th, 1914.

1001 Flight Sub-Lieut. Kenneth Falshaw Watson, R.N.A.S. (Grahame - White Biplane, Grahame - White School, Hendon). Dec. 19th, 1914.

1002 Maurice Leigh Gardner (Wright Biplane, Beatty School, Hendon). Dec. 20th, 1914.

Re-election of Members.—It was unanimously resolved :—

"That the Members elected between the 1st November, 1913, and the 31st October, 1914, be re-elected under Rule 39, except those who are alien enemies."

Flying Services Fund.—It was reported that at the Special General Meeting held that afternoon the motion "That the Club contribute £1,000 to the Flying Services Fund" was carried, the voting being 20 in favour and 11 against.

It was decided that the Fund should be known as "The Flying Services Fund."

Further consideration of the matter was deferred until the next meeting of the Committee on Wednesday, the 30th inst.

Aero Club of America.—The following letter from the Aero Club of America was received :—

"December 8th, 1914.

"The President, Royal Aero Club, 166, Piccadilly, London, W.

"SIR,—The following resolution, expressing our sympathy for the affiliated clubs of the Fédération Aéronautique Internationale, was unanimously adopted at the annual meeting of the Aero Club of America, held on November 9th, 1914 :—

"Whereas : in the great European conflict the ranks of our sister clubs of the Fédération Aéronautique Internationale have been thinned as the result of the daring of their members who have given patriotic service to their countries at the cost of

The Aero Club magazine: note the Leeds flyer, (name boxed) Kenneth Watson.
Author's collection

the trenches, and Kenneth Watson, a rugby player, was a flight lieutenant in the Royal Navy Air Service. He was reported missing after a flight over the sea, in August. His parents in Headingley had received the unwelcome telegram. Watson had left base on patrol duties and had not returned. He had been trained at Hendon, in the Graham-White School, and had qualified for the Royal Aero Club in December 1914.

One of these sports stars, Evelyn Lintott, was with the Leeds Pals, and by December 1915, those men were at the Suez Canal, having sailed from home on a tough voyage through the Mediterranean. Turkey, now an ally of Germany, made an attempt to take the strategically important Suez Canal, which was not only important as a Mediterranean base, but was vital in the route taken by the Indian Army when they reinforced the British regiments at war. Lintott was a teacher and a footballer, and had played for Bradford City before joining Leeds City (as they were named before being 'United') in 1912. He enlisted in the Leeds Pals in September 1914, and with his battalion he was in Egypt in the December of that year. The men were encamped at Port Said at one time, and were on guard at a crucially important strategic position. Laurie Milner, in his detailed history of the Pals, reproduced several diary entries from some of the men based there, and we have a picture of the men at work and play, now wearing their pith helmets and desert gear. There were some pleasant aspects to this, as this extract from Lieutenant Bickersteth's diary shows: 'The whole battalion parades as strong as possible and marches down to the beach; there they divest themselves of all clothes and bathe. The water is beautifully warm and by 11 o'clock the sun is really hot.'

There was not only the canal to be guarded, but a railway too. Anyone who has read T.E. Lawrence's classic, *The Seven Pillars of Wisdom*, will recall the attacks on the Turkish railways, which were essential for the movement of troops, of course. The 'railway war' extended to the Middle East as well as France and Flanders. Clearly, there was going to be some 'action' with such precious locations and assets to protect. Laurie Milner puts it neatly: 'Soon after their arrival, the Pals fired their first shots in anger.' He quotes Clifford Hollingworth, who wrote an extensive account of his experiences in the war: 'Well, Taffy Jones and Denton Rogers were on sentry duty and you used to walk 50 yards in front of the post on the railway and his train come, and it wouldn't stop at midnight, and they fired on it.'

They moved from base camp to base camp, and the desert storms appear to have been worse causes of fear than the enemy. But all infantry

A scene on the Suez Canal, just after the war. *Author's collection*

A near contemporary map showing the Suez region. *Phillips, 1928*

PAVING THE WAY FOR THE GUNS,

A scene from the war in the desert. *Author's collection*

wars are packed with the undesirable activity of digging in, and the Pals did plenty of that. The whole expedition proved to be, essentially, an extension of training, as it involved new skills and the plentiful practice of acquired ones. Laurie Milner gives an account of arguably one of the worst experiences that any soldier may have – the accidental killing of a fellow fighter. This happened on this Suez trip, when Private Prince accidentally shot Edward Wintle. Naturally, there was a very awkward and uneasy situation, and Wintle's funeral took place at Kantara. Milner recalls that Prince was court-martialled, and he sums up the response, noting that some degree of humanity was exerted, when the initial punishment of twenty-eight days of Field Punishment Number 2 (being strapped to a stationary object) was reduced to seven days.

As for the Pals and their war – the Somme awaited them the following year.

Where was God in the middle of all this suffering? A year after the outbreak of war, with the first great swathes of horrific statistics of death and maiming of men, the church felt that something ritualistic was needed. Leeds did what every city did: from 30 July to 1 August there were services and speeches, with solemn music and prayer. It must have seemed as if the people back home needed some kind of reassurance, because the usual questions were being asked – why did the good Creator of this world allow such mass death and suffering to happen? On 30 July, at Kirkstall Abbey, as *The Yorkshire Post* described, the first gathering for prayer happened: 'In view of the solemn thoughts which occur to one as the anniversary of the day of Declaration of War draws near, it was peculiarly appropriate that in an atmosphere of simple greatness … Leeds people should have had the opportunity to meet together to pray.'

Then, on the afternoon of 1 August, there was a grand service. Just before that, the press recalled a letter from the Vicar of Leeds, Dr Bickersteth, on 14 July, referring to a series of speeches from different religious leaders, made at the Town Hall. Bickersteth's words are typical of the ideology of the time, which reinforced the view that Britain was fighting a righteous war, with God on its side. Bickersteth wrote that people should 'take to heart the call from God to our empire, and to all Europe, to repent, to renew its faith in Him, in His judgements and His mercies, and to ask for His grace to fight on patiently to the finish'.

This was a year before the Battle of the Somme. Those who read Bickersteth's words that summer would have had some difficulties grasping the implications of the phrase 'to repent' because conventional thinking could place war in the category of something that could expiate sin. Strangely, that notion, expressed as 'sacrifice' and 'cleansing', was built into the literature and thinking about the war. The popular magazines often depicted Tommies as 'sacrificing' their futures for the force of good. One magazine carried a feature on officers in the army seen as 'the new knights' – Lancelots facing the dark forces of evil.

From today's standpoint, some might read all this as indoctrination, but we have to look at 1915 on its own terms. The fact is that Leeds people saw their march to war as a force supporting goodness and truly human qualities, as opposed to the brutality of the Germans, clearly indicated in the Belgian atrocities.

Towards the end of the year, munitions were top priority. Leeds was really in the forefront in this respect. In July, *The Yorkshire Post* noted:

> In response to a request from the Ministry of Munitions, classes for engineering workshop instructors started today. Many local men and women have offered their services for the making of ammunition, but the authorities have been obliged to refuse them, firstly because they were not trained for this kind of work, and secondly because part-time labour is out of the question in the present emergency.

In October 1914, a Shells Committee had been formed, and it took six meetings for arrangements to be made for the government to underwrite the cost of expanding some armament works. Kitchener was opposed

Inside a shell shop run by the railways. *Author's collection*

on many points. But on 5 March 1915, a new Munitions Committee, with Lloyd George as director, was created and things started moving. Unfortunately, in April of this year, the Prime Minister, Asquith, was to make a faux pas at a speech in Newcastle. He wrote in a letter that he had had a talk with Sir John French, and 'He [French] told me that I could let you [Venetia Stanley] know that with the present supply of munitions he will have as much as his troops will be able to use on the next forward movement.' He then told the munitions workers in Newcastle, 'I do not believe that any army … has ever entered upon a campaign with better or more adequate equipment.' Michael Brock, editing Asquith's letters, commented that this was 'the most damaging blunder of his wartime premiership'.

It was clearly one of the many reasons why production had to be stepped up; hence the Barnbow development.

In December, the Barnbow munitions factory was beginning work, after a long preparation, and more will be said on this in the account of 1916. It must be noted that in the summer of that year, the national press were full of praise for the Leeds effort in answering the call to increase munitions production. *The Times* special correspondent wrote, in June:

> What is being done in Leeds seems to me of particular interest because it bears upon one of the root causes of the labour difficulty. They have taken the best course to avoid any. They are concentrating their energies on a special shell factory, in which, I understand, complete shells will be produced. The factory is being prepared under the direction of a small executive committee of engineering employers. ... This is what is meant by a 'national factory'.

As will be seen, with hindsight, that special project was doomed to lead to a terrible disaster. But just a few months after Barnbow was opened, a small note in the local press gave a hint of the pressure involved in meeting targets: 'To meet the increased demands of the War Office, they were doubling the area and equipment of their factory. They had got their second new factory in a forward state and they expected in another ten weeks they would require another thousand men.'

Christmas week this year brought out the spirit of celebration and fun wherever it could be achieved in between all the hard work and commitment to the cause. At Beckett Park Hospital, for instance, as *The Yorkshire Post* commented, 'The cheerfulness and jollity of our soldiers under the most trying conditions is one of the things that strike all observers, and in hospital, their good spirits never fail them.' The Christmas celebration began with the choir of St Michael's, Headingley, who went to the hospital and walked the wards, singing as they went. Then Santa Claus paid a visit on Christmas morning. The whole business was designated a festival, and patients joined nurses in decorating the wards and corridors. There was a Holy Communion and a church parade, and the press noted that 'the big assembly hall was especially pretty'.

Of course, there were theatricals as well. At Roundhay Auxiliary Hospital, after divine service, folk did what they had always loved: the men gave a tableaux show, and that evening in the Gledhow Hall Hospital they had a theatrical performance to enjoy.

At Killingbeck, there was turkey and plum pudding, and a 'special' tea, which involved a concert by the staff, with a feast of popular song. Theatre was even more special at the East Leeds Military Hospital, because artistes from the Grand Theatre gave a show, and patients had bulky stockings on their beds, full of useful underwear and a pipe for every man.

There was also a notable advance in the YMCA provision in December that year. No survey of the Great War support facilities is complete without mention of the YMCA. There was widespread support for the work of this organization, which by the time of war had four bases in Yorkshire, with sixty-eight workers. The working of the Association was rather similar in spirit to the London settlements for the poor: that is, students participated, and it fulfilled that great ideal of service to others that was inspiring many in the middle classes in that generation born in the 1880s and 1890s. When the war demanded much more of them in the military camps, fundraising accelerated rapidly. After all, this is a British affair we are describing, and that being so, the cheeriness went as far as amateur dramatics wherever possible, as this letter from Frank Isherwood shows:

> We went yesterday to see the Fourth Division Follies, they are a party of Pierrots got up by the motor ambulance people. The first part of the performance, consisting of songs in the 'folly' manner … In the interval, one of them came in front of the curtain and told stories. One of them was about the Bishop whose wife wrote a book and also had a child and when a gushing lady complimented him about the child he thought she meant the book and said, 'Wasn't it clever of her – she did it all by herself, she got no help from me and certainly no help from the Archdeacon!'

Clearly, the whole enterprise of voluntary work, being not only to treat the troops but also to cheer them, was one of the great success stories of the war (note the reference 'got up by the ambulance people').

Regarding the YMCA and their key role in this widespread support, they just grew, like Topsy: in 1918, there were fifty-five YMCA huts in Yorkshire. One writer described the YMCA work in its essential role:

> The YMCA followed troops to the front line and to the sites of conflict scattered across the globe – for this was truly a world war. As the wounded returned so the YMCA found itself working alongside the Royal Army Medical Corps in hospitals and convalescent homes, and in helping relatives to visit their sons. It also began to provide for the thousands of munitions workers housed in camps scattered around the country. By 1917 the YMCAs were responsible for 150 munitions workers' canteens, serving c.200,000 workers daily.

It would not be too much to insist that the YMCA grew to be a crucially important point of contact for men either in the field or in transit, at

A scene showing where the first help and support would be behind the lines. *Author's collection*

home or abroad: the hut or base – of any kind – was a symbol of reassurance, asserting values of comfort and support in a world that must have seemed to many to be placed just next door to hell.

Up to the end of June 1915, the institution in Albion Place supplied home comforts to all men seeking refuge when passing through the city, but by that time the accommodation was found inadequate … but in December …they opened premises in Albion Street which were especially serviceable to men arriving at the railway stations who required a night's lodging or a few hours' rest, recreation and refreshment during the day. Here they received the personal attention of lady helpers, some 250 of whom had volunteered for the duties.

Success in this initiative is not hard to ascertain: a record of five months' work showed that there were 845 attendances; workers met 2,401 trains and dealt with 5,180 men. One estimate was that the total number of clients for the YMCA in Albion Street was about 2 million. In every phase of the war, in the ways in which Leeds was affected, there were personnel passing through. Many would be on their way to the Ripon or Colsterdale camps; others would need to be helped to the numerous military hospitals. There would also be a fair number of those who were simply lost and displaced.

If one has to find one skill that was quintessentially British at this time it was caring for those who were casualties of war – whether they were wounded physically, suffering from mental stress, or simply caught in the confusing trajectory of the process of a world war moving relentlessly and mercilessly towards its conclusion.

The year was, in the words of W.H. Scott, summed up by the phrase 'tightening the belt', and it entailed, on the home front, continuous fundraising efforts. One of the outstanding examples of this was the Flag Day Collection. This began in July and the cash was specifically garnered to be used to support the Leeds men in action at the front. The operation was simple – it involved street collections, which could be undertaken by anyone. Collecting boxes were distributed to factories, places of entertainment, pubs and anywhere where people would gather. Much of the street collecting was done by children.

Above and beyond these particular initiatives, there was the basic groundwork of adapting to wartime exigencies. Largely this was concerned with leisure and recreation (or the lack of it), controlling food supplies, and regulating transport movements. Everything that could be used as a location for training, testing or storing was utilized. A typical example was the beautiful open space of Roundhay Park, which was used for military drilling as well as such matters as the testing of aircraft. Scott points out that some of the most dense retail areas – he chooses Roundhay Road, which was a mass of well-stocked shops with multi-cultural presence as late as the 1960s – were affected. He wrote, 'Confectioners, in accordance with regulations, refrained from tempting purchasers by exhibits of sweetstuffs in the windows; the few shown were but samples, as many a vendor was careful to explain. "No chocolates" was a very common notice.'

By the end of the first year of war, as statistics compiled in 1922 show, Leeds's military contribution had been assessed in twelve categories (as at July, 1915), from the 12,362 men of Kitchener's Army and the almost 6,000 Leeds Pals, down to the University Officer Training Corps, which had recruited 360 men by that time. As Scott sums up, 'At the beginning of January 1915, the 20,000 mark had been passed; at the end of April the figures reached 30,000, and three months later, a total of over 36,000 was recorded, including 2,000 Regulars.'

Chapter Three

1916: The Conflict Intensifies

At the beginning of the year, the first Military Service Act was passed, bringing in conscription for unmarried men aged from eighteen to forty-one. Exceptions were for widowers with children, ministers of religion, or men in reserved occupations. In May, the conscription was extended to include married men. Anyone claiming exemption from this had to face a formidable tribunal.

At first, during the debates on the imminent war in early August 1914, those who argued for conscription did so with only home defence in their thoughts. The growth of the German navy and the advent of the Zeppelins lay behind this attitude. Historians Michael and Eleanor Brock point out, with reference to Lord Northcliffe, who was a press and publishing magnate and a powerful voice in the formation of opinion, that he 'was opposed sending a single British soldier to the Continent.' In that atmosphere, when the talk was all of the German atrocities against 'Little Belgium', as the Brocks add further, conscription was almost a dirty word. 'Conscription was the touchstone. In the changed mood the impression grew that the Cabinet were refusing to prepare for it, not because it would be impractical, but because their whole past made them revolt against this kind of compulsion.' How different things were to be two years later. But in the meantime, men rushed to join up.

In Leeds there were a number of war resisters, or conscientious objectors, as they came to be called, and of course the Quakers were prominent among these. In the city a major figure in this was Thomas Harvey, born in Leeds, the eldest son of William Harvey, who was a prominent art collector who also worked on the Leeds City Council for thirteen years. Thomas became MP for the city (Leeds West) in December 1910. Harvey was a pacifist, but contrary to popular belief, not all Friends (Quakers) were against the war; some accepted the notion of a 'just war' and fought, or worked in non-combatant roles. Harvey contributed by working for the War Victims' Relief Committee created by the Quakers. He and Arnold Rowntree, another Quaker, played a part in the composition of the section of the new Act that paid attention to the definition of 'work of national importance', which was part of exemption classification. This was not popular with some in the ranks of the conscientious objectors who became known as Absolutists, as they would not do any work connected with war. A further contentious aspect of Harvey's work in this context was that he took part in the Pelham Committee, which worked out measures to provide work for the Absolutists (who were at that point all in prison). This became known as the Home Office Scheme, and in most cases this led to experiences for the objectors that were in many ways even worse than their suffering at the hands of the prison regimes they knew.

In this context of pacifist activism, there was also Maurice Rowntree, who became prominent in the Swarthmore Settlement in Leeds, which was an adult education centre. He was educated at Oxford, and took a lectureship at Swarthmore. The centre was described by one writer in the 1920s: 'The students are to a large extent working men who have proved themselves keenly interested in a wide range of subjects.' Rowntree was active also in work at a temperance café in one of the city's poorer districts.

Maurice had to face a tribunal, of course. He was given twenty-one days in which to find some work of national importance: his work in education and in helping the poor was not considered to be important. Back he went to the second tribunal, and this time he was arrested and court-martialled. His destination was Wormwood Scrubs prison in London, where hundreds of conscientious objectors were held. The point here is that men were deemed to be soldiers, under the Military Service Acts. Even if they said that they refused to join and to fight, it made no difference. They were defined as soldiers and were subject to a court martial.

Maurice gave a rousing speech later, in 1917, and made his presence felt at the Scarborough Free Church Council. A resolution was passed, and he had made his mark. But in his 'criminal' career he was always courageous. His statement when at the police court has been summarized by one historian, and it expresses the war resister attitudes:

He thought he was called upon, with what effort and strength he had, to work with a view to a different order of life, and a different way of settling disputes altogether. In doing that he felt it became of international importance. … He held in detestation the infamous actions of Germany. He wished them to be clear about that. But he thought that really war would never bring peace, except the peace of death.

THE ALTERNATIVE.

Better barren women than children bred for war,
Better death in birth than manhood trained for murder ;
Better bleak wild country than shattered flesh and bone ;
Better voided earth before Primeval Sundawn ;
And better dead blank world if battles still must rage—
        But best of all no war at all,
        And Peace in a Golden Age.

                                        C. G. C.

A cartoon illustrating the need for joining up. *Author's collection*

The initial massive recruitment of 1914 and the creation of the Pals battalions had happened on the crest of a wave of enthusiasm for the war; Germany would have to pay – for the moral outrage of what had been perpetrated against Belgium and France, and also for the unspeakable effrontery of actually bombing English towns. That militarization had occurred within a context of a hatred of conscription; the notion was that going to war was assuredly something that a free-born Brit did willingly, for moral reasons. The enthusiasm was sustained throughout the end of 1914 and into the first four months or so of 1915, but then came the mass deaths of the battles resulting from the need to keep Ypres and the coastal towns, and that entailed huge losses in the ranks of the professional soldiers, which had been disturbingly high since the very first encounters with the powerful German armies in the last months of 1914.

When the new men of Kitchener's Army finally arrived in France and faced battle for the first time, the shock of such high casualty rates began to hit home. By the end of 1915 it became clear to the War Office that more recruitment was needed. The solution was the Derby Scheme. Under this, men attested with a signed certificate, agreeing to enlist when called. Naturally, many thought that the war would be over before they were called, but they were wrong.

John Graham, the official historian of the No-Conscription Fellowship, a group that had been formed in 1914, put the situation strongly: 'The War Office had drained the country of all willing men who could be at all reasonably spared.' But it was now represented to be a choice between defeat and a force so vastly increased that conscription was the only way to collect it. Derby's attestation was in effect a compiled register. First, unmarried men from eighteen to forty-one were called; then later married men were included. As Graham put it, 'The nation had come to believe that every available man must be compelled to join up.'

In Leeds, as was the case everywhere, there were hundreds of tribunals reported, and their nature ranged from the tragic to the farcical. One wealthy man claimed exception for his chauffeur, as his first chauffeur had been called up, and without his car he would actually have had to walk a short distance to catch a train into the city.

The situation with the tribunals and the determined effort to enforce conscription whenever possible was further stirred and fomented by the national and regional press. *The Yorkshire Post*, for instance, in December 1915, when the topic of attestation and the 'Derby Men' was hot news, made no mistake that it saw a certain group in the Leeds community who were not pulling their weight:

It is no use blinking the fact that the bachelors of Roundhay, Chapeltown and Headingley, particularly those between twenty and thirty years of age, stand exposed as a race apart from the patriotic Englishman. The rich and the poor have proved their mettle, but I regret to say that the single men in a great number of middle-class families have shown themselves to be shirkers. It is the middle classes who have brought the country to the need for compulsion.

There was a great deal of business for the tribunals. The fine details of the administration in force, and of the delays and frustrations involved, are evident in this extract from a major feature in early 1916:

> Priestley Hall is still open for men who were attested in the last two days under the group system to fill in their attestation papers, and receive their pay, but the Oxford Row depot is closed. Men who joined at Oxford Row and Albert Hall must now apply for their papers and pay at the Central Recruiting Office. Captain Hill, Senior Recruiting Officer in Leeds, requests the heads of those firms to forward him another list of their employees who come under the five groups. … If any man is still not in possession of a white card [attestation form] the employer should state whether he is married or single.

There is a sense, while reading this, that there are plenty of men in the shadows, thinking and waiting, very nervously, hoping that delay and

A list of the conscientious objectors who died in jail. Note the name 'Moss … Morley'. *No-Conscription Fellowship, 1919*

THE MEN WHO DIED

The following sixty-nine comrades died after arrest, the first ten while in prison

E, WALTER - - -	BIRKENHEAD	
)LE, O. S. - - -	BRIGHTON	
NS, E. - - -	FAILSWORTH	
LER, A. - - -	STOCKPORT	
PBELL, P. - - -	ISLE OF SKYE	
AN, P. L. - - -	LONDON	
TON, A. - - -	MANCHESTER	
KINSON, F. - -	DULWICH	
SON, A. - - -	BLACKBURN	
TER, J. G. - -	CORNSAY	
EN, PETER - - -	NELSON	
EN, TOM - - -	NELSON	
EN, WALTER G. -	NEW SOUTHGATE	
LOW, A. - - -	MANSFIELD WOODHOUSE	
ENHAM, F. - -	DOWNHAM MARKET	
NON, H. - - -	SWANSEA	
DEN, F. - - -	OLDHAM	
NTNALL, A. G. -	LONDON	
HTMAN, H. - -	CAMDEN TOWN	
EY, THOMAS - -	MANCHESTER	
PBELL, N. A. -	GLASGOW	
, C. J. - - -	CROYDON	
OIS, G. H - -	RISCA	
LER, L. - - -	WEST BROMPTON	
BERY, P. - -	BLACKBURN	
GBLUT, A. - -	LONDON, N.W.	
IS, J. L. - -	CARDIFF	
IS, R. G. - -	READING	
H, H. W. - -	NORWICH	
LDSBOROUGH, H. -	BLACKBURN	
, PERCY - - -	OLD DALBY	
ON, H. - - -	CHESTERFIELD	
DERSON, A. - -	DUNDEE	
ST, A. - - -	SOUTHWARK	
HOAD, H. - - -	CHART SUTTON	
HOOPER, R. - -	BRADFORD	
HURLEY, W. - -	CAMBERWELL	
HURST, H. - -	MANCHESTER	
JACKSON, THEODORE		
JAMES, A. L. - -	KINGSTON	
JAMES, H. - -	WORCESTER	
LINSCOTT, S. - -	NEWTON ABBOT	
MALCOLM, W. W. -	GLASGOW	
MARTLEW, A. - -	YORK	
MATCHETT, T. D. -	BATH	
MAY, W. - - -	EDINBURGH	
MOSS, — - - -	MORLEY	
MOUNTFIELD, J. -	MANCHESTER	
PARKIN, W. H. -	SHEFFIELD	
PARTON, F. L. -	CHISWICK	
PEDDIESON, A. -	GLASGOW	
PHIPPS, H. - -	HARRINGAY	
RICHMOND, R. A. -	BRIGHTON	
RIGG, J. A. - -	BARROW-IN-FURNESS	
ROBERTS, W. L. -	STOCKPORT	
RUDALL, A. - -	NEWPORT	
SLATER, A. J. -	GLASGOW	
STAFFORD, N. -	HYDE	
STANTON, W. -	LEICESTER	
STATTON, — - -	CARDIFF	
SWETTENHAM, W. -	LIVERPOOL	
TAYLOR, J. - -	SILVERTOWN	
THOMPSON, C. -	NORWICH	
TODD, G. - - -	WILLESDEN	
WALLACE, B. -	NEWMARKET	
WHINNERAH, G. -	BARROW-IN-FURNESS	
WHILMORE, P. A. -	COVENTRY	
WOODWARD, E. -	BIRMINGHAM	
ZACHNIES, C. -	GLASGOW	

prevarication will save the day. After all, as the tribunals make very clear, men conscripted were likely to lose their families and their business, such were the harsh attitudes of the majority of tribunals towards claims for exemption.

Those who had attested and had to provide visible evidence of the fact that they were ready to fight could wear an armlet. But even that had its problems. Around Christmas 1915, the *Yorkshire Evening Post* had done some research on the tendency for a number of men not to wear the armlet. The paper sent a man out to search for opinion, and he found lots of reasons for the refusal:

The armlet is an ugly and inartistic one.
It is difficult to prevent the band from slipping off the sleeve.
It is nothing but 'swank' to wear one.
It is too wide, and the red crown too prominent.
It attracts attention, and makes a man feel self-conscious.

Of course, the alternative was to risk receiving a white feather in a matchbox – the allegation of cowardice.

There was a constant awareness that evidence of commitment to the war had to be visible. One anonymous Tommy recorded this in his diary, for instance, in June 1916:

17. Fell out and went sick with blistered feet after which went to Sutton, half afraid that I should be stopped and accused of malingering.

18. Went for a route march and attended bathing parade. On the march the boys were very busy asking all the young chaps why they weren't in khaki. Greengrocers threw fruit at us but they soon got tired of that.

As the tribunals went on, there were more and more ridiculous cases heard by the board of members. A typically amusing one is the case of the mole catcher. On 24 March, before the Leeds Military Service Tribunal, a mole catcher stood as applicant for exemption, and this was a busy day: there were sixty-two cases to consider. *The Yorkshire Post* reported this dialogue:

'The only one in Leeds,' was the claim of a mole catcher who applied for exemption on the grounds that his services were of a nature indispensable to agriculture. He submitted a list of the farms which he 'worked' and admitted that his employment brought in a very fair income.

Chairman: 'What do you do with the moles when you have caught them?'

Applicant: 'I skin them and sell the skins.'

Chairman: 'So you have a double event on this – you get paid for catching them and then get money for the skins?'

Applicant (smiling): 'Yes.'

The appeal was dismissed.

In early June that year, a young man called Barbellion wrote this entry in his diary:

> This morning in bed I heard a man with a milk cart say in the road to a villager at about 6.30 am, 'battle … and we lost six cruisers.' This was the first I knew of the Battle of Jutland. At 8.00 am I read in the *Daily News* that the British navy had been defeated, and thought it was the end of all things. The news took away our appetites. At the railway station the *Morning Post* was more cheerful, even reassuring, and now at 6.30 pm the battle has turned into a merely regrettable indecisive action. We breathe once more.

As this hints, Jutland was big news. The German fleet had been penned in, tight, in the Baltic ports, by the British navy for some time. Then, at the end of May, the Germans turned and attacked the British, commanded by Sir John Jellicoe. It was not exactly a significant result for Britain. One summary of the British Grand Fleet has this criticism: 'The Grand Fleet's rangefinders were deficient, its target-plotting machinery prone to error, and its gunnery computers, staff work and armoured protection defective.'

This was the Battle of Jutland, in the last days of May that year. There had been a continuing war in the North Sea, since the beginning of hostilities, when German mines had been laid, Grimsby trawlers had been converted to minesweepers, and the Royal Navy set up reservist bodies and support men of all kinds to match the menace from the sea. The British Grand Fleet was pitted against the German High Seas Fleet in skirmish after skirmish, and Jutland became arguably the most memorable encounter. Admiral Beatty managed to trap the Germans, and should have demolished them, but technology let the Royal Navy down, as target-plotting equipment did not function properly, and there were defects in gunnery computers as well as in armoured protection.

In contrast, the German guns were effective. In the end, there were heavy British losses, but the result was indecisive. There were terrible casualty figures recorded, and several Leeds men were in these figures. Some examples have been given after family history research, such as the case of Louis Nowland, who lived in Clara Street in Leeds. He served on the *Queen Mary* at Jutland, where a German shell hit the ship's magazines and the whole vessel was split. There had possibly been damage from the ship's own shells, of course, after that type of hit.

We know quite a lot about that action, as we have reports from survivors, such as these memories from Midshipman Storey:

> The fire was maintained with great rapidity till 5.20, and during this time we were only slightly damaged by the enemy's fire. At 5.20 a big shell hit 'Q' turret and put the right gun out of action, but the left gun continued firing. At 5.24 a terrific explosion took place which smashed up 'Q' turret and started a big fire in a working chamber, and the gun house was filled with smoke and gas. The officer on the turret, Lieutenant Commander Street, gave the order to evacuate the turret … another terrific explosion took place and we were all thrown into the water. On coming to the surface, nothing was visible except wreckage, but thirty persons appeared to be floating in the water.

Twenty-one men survived, with several being severely wounded.

Then, in the summer, came the quintessential character of trench warfare, and the Leeds Pals were to play a part in that horror. When many of the first volunteer recruits had started their soldier careers, they had been billeted in huts, as was the case at Colsterdale. Now, the Pals were based on the fields of France, and in July, they were involved in one of the greatest battles in military history: the Somme.

Modern readers need to be reminded at this point of the nature of the soldier's experience, with regard to what is now in the history books, in contradistinction to what the actual conflict was like. Peter Fiennes has expressed this very well in his biography of his padre grandfather:

> To them it was a series of assaults, a relentless sleep-starved struggle against the constant bombardment of shells, shrapnel and gas amongst wire and machine guns, bombs and mortars. In that squalor of mud and rain, they met dread and terror, and found themselves capable of unimaginable heroism. It was only those in charge who saw the larger picture.

The master plan of the British was to confront the enemy along a line of about 16 miles, taking some of the pressure of the prolonged fight off the French armies at Verdun. The offensive in its first phase was led by Sir Henry Rawlinson, the man who had conceived the notion of the 'Pals' battalions, with thirteen divisions of the Fourth Army. The Pals were in the reserve line.

One soldier of the artillery, in an anonymous journal, described the moment before the battle began:

> Sat 1 July. Today the big attack on the Germans commenced. Reveille was at 4.00 am. At 8.00 am the battery turned out in full marching order and paraded on the gun park, hooked into the limbers ready to move off if the infantry advance was sufficiently successful. … Everyone was keenly excited and expectant for now 'open warfare' was anticipated and the beginning of the end.

John Buchan, the writer of one of the first officially sanctioned accounts of the Somme, explained the root of the massive and demanding warfare that was to come from July onwards through to November:

> Now to quote a famous saying of General Foch, 'A weakening force must always be attacking,' and from the beginning of 1916 the Central Powers [Germans and friends] were forced into a continuous offensive. Their economic strength was draining rapidly. Their people had been told that victory was already won. … They feared greatly the coming Allied offensive, for they knew that it would be simultaneous on all fronts.

Leeds men from a number of regiments were involved in the Somme, of course. It was a battle that was to take its name from the river Somme, and the beginning of this offensive lay in General Haig's desire to launch a huge attack and take the main line of German trenches very quickly, believing that a sustained artillery bombardment before the infantry moved would win the day. He was wrong. The infantry advance brought his force almost 60,000 casualties on the first day of July. The enemy trenches had been made of sterner stuff, being dug deeply in the ground and made of sturdy material. The British moved against lines of machine guns. And there was slaughter. July did bring its heroes, though, in that horrendous place. One of Leeds's most outstanding participants in the war won his Victoria Cross in this month: this was George Sanders of the 7th Battalion, West Yorkshire Regiment, and he won the honour at Thiepval. The citation reads:

> Corporal Sanders and thirty men found themselves isolated after an advance into enemy trenches. He organized his defences, detailed his men and impressed upon them to hold their position at all costs. Next morning he drove off an attack, rescuing some prisoners who had fallen into enemy hands. Two further bombing attacks were

resisted. He was relieved after thirty-six hours. His party had been without food and water, having given their water to the wounded.

Sanders died in 1950, and was buried at Cottingley Crematorium.

The Pals were in the thick of battle not long after arriving in France from Egypt. They were soon accustomed to the demands of trench warfare, and they lost their first man in France when Corporal Frank Bygott was shot – yet another accidental death. They were in the front line before July, and there were losses, including that of their first officer – Lieutenant James Wardle, from Headingley. He died a few days after being wounded. The Leeds papers provided a steady stream of obituaries, with photographs. In May and June they were shifted around, with regular casualties, and one note, by Private Cosby, sums up the gruelling time they were having: '22 May 1916 – a terrible night. Front trenches shelled for over an hour. Bat. suffers greatest losses so far – about fifty casualties. Bombardment took place about 10.30. An unforgettable experience.'

There are plenty of remarkable stories from this phase in the battalion's life, but one in particular has been the subject of numerous press features in the centenary year of 2014 – that of Private Jogendra N. Sen. He was from Bengal, and had been a student at the University of Leeds since 1910, studying for a BSc degree. Later he worked at the Leeds Corporation Electric Lighting Station in Whitehall Road. The obituary in *The Yorkshire Post* on 2 June notes that he 'came in for much notice because of his evident connection with the east'. We have a real insight into the ethics of the times in these words of Arthur Dalby to Laurie Milner, on Sen: 'He was the best educated man in the battalion and he spoke about seven languages but he was never allowed to be not even a lance corporal because in those days they would never let a coloured fellow be over a white man.'

We know from a letter written by Private Burniston how Sen died: 'He was hit in the leg and neck by shrapnel and died almost immediately. He was evidently hit in the leg first as when they fetched him in he had a bandage tied round it.'

On the very first day of the offensive, 1 July, Evelyn Lintott, the Leeds footballer referred to in the previous chapter, was killed. It happened in the scrap at Serre, which was the place the Pals had been ordered to take. Buchan describes the context:

The divisions in action there [between Gommecourt and Thiepval] were mainly from the New Army. ... They had to face a chain of fortified villages – Gommecourt, Serre, Beaumont Hamel and

Thiepval – and enemy positions which were generally on higher and better ground. … Each village had been so fortified so as to be impregnable.

Lintott was shot in the chest. *The Yorkshire Post* reported, 'He led his men with great dash and when hit the first time declined to take the count. Instead, he drew his revolver and called for further effort. Again he was hit but struggled on, but a third shot finally bowled him over.'

There were other famous sportsmen in the casualty lists too, such as Roy Kilner, a cricketer, who was hit exactly where a bowler would dread it – in the wrist. But he was a left-hand bowler and his wound was on the right wrist.

In ten minutes, as Derek Fraser, writing about the battle, put it, C and D companies of the Leeds Pals were destroyed. He adds, 'One officer, no sergeant majors, and only forty-seven of the 800 NCOs and men survived the attack.'

One diary kept by a Leeds man gives a poignant series of statements that reflect the terrible summer of that year:

6 July Battle of the Somme. German casualties heavy. West Yorkshire soldiers' valour.

8 July Leeds Pals Battalion suffered severely in the Battle of the Somme. Heavy casualties. How they went into action.

26 July The stricken brave. Leeds soldiers killed. Thirty-four photos printed.

5 August Leeds Grammar School Speech Day. Mr Wynne-Edwards said the school had sent out over 600 men to fight the country's battles, and of these nearly 300 were new officers.

19 August Leeds soldiers killed. Thirty more photos.

As the battle wore on, as well as the horrendous lists of the dead and wounded, there were other stories of heroism. On 27 October, there was another VC. This was Fred McNess of the Scots Guards. He was extremely brave, fighting on while severely injured. The biography is a tragic one, as the wounds he sustained left him with intolerable pain, and eventually he was to take his own life.

A picture of the VC winner Fred McNess.

His citation is as follows:

> On 15 September near Ginchy, France, during a period of severe fighting Lance Sergeant McNess led his men with great dash in the face of heavy shell and machine-gun fire. When the first line of the enemy trenches was reached, it was found that the left flank was exposed and that the enemy were bombing down the trench. McNess thereupon organized and led a counter-attack and although he was severely wounded in the neck and jaw, did not give up. Finally he established a 'block' and continued encouraging his men and throwing bombs until exhausted by loss of blood.

He did progress from lance sergeant to full sergeant after that, and who would argue with that? He deserved every honour that could be given.

Then there was George Sanders, another VC winner. He had been to Little Holbeck School and then worked as a fitter at the Airedale foundry. He enlisted in November 1914 into the Prince of Wales's Own Regiment, 7th Battalion. It was at Thiepval that he found that he had been cut off with just a small group of men. He then did what military leaders have done down the centuries – dug in and organized things. He had a bombing party and well-founded defences. Then they gritted their teeth and stayed put. The small band then repelled an enemy advance and even rescued some prisoners. The Sanders group had done this without food and water. Sanders took his VC from King George on 18 November 1916 at Buckingham Palace. We will hear of him again in 1918.

Sanders, a Leeds VC hero.

At home, the show had to go on – and that meant the entertainment industry as well. Leeds had for a very long time been a place notable for theatre, variety and music of all kinds. The famous composer Arthur Sullivan had many times been asked to write for the Leeds festivals and various musical celebrations. The theatres were well established on the circuit of the variety artistes. There were also the 'pictures' and at the Leeds Empire there was a typical piece of propaganda, as one report described, 'a film called *Britain Prepared* was shown … a series of pictures calculated to impress the mind with the immense efforts required to enable the country to play its part worthily in the world war.' The Lord Mayor attended, said the report, and he made a speech in which 'he would remind them that it was not necessary for every man who helped in the war to take part in military operations. There were many sick and wounded to be attended to at the front.'

The Grand then, as now, was the pride of the city for more serious theatre and music. It had been opened in 1878, with a production of *Much Ado about Nothing*, and in the later Victorian years, such major stars as Lillie Langtry and Sarah Bernhardt had appeared there. In the year before the war, there was a truly memorable production there – Wagner's massive opera, *The Ring of the Nibelung*. Then, in the war, again, patriotic pieces were common, such as *Sealed Orders*, which was described as a 'great naval and patriotic play'.

On 23 December 1916, *The Leeds Mercury* ran a profile of Miss Doris Halton. The headline was 'Munition Worker's Feat' and the piece went on to describe how Miss Halton pierced 70,000 cartridges in a day at Greenwood and Batley's cartridge factory in Leeds. The machine she used pierced holes in the cap chamber of the cartridge, and her achievement was impressive. Another worker wrote to tell the paper, 'Our reason for sending you this record is to show that some of us are doing our bit here in Leeds, and also to silence some of the pessimistic croakers.' The women's work with the cartridges was explained: 'The operation is one which requires exceptional deftness of the fingers, for each case has to be separately handled and inserted into a perforated plate which is constantly revolving and … the piercing machines are very fragile.' Miss Halton was only seventeen.

However, what the readers of that feature did not know is that a few weeks before, at Barnbow munitions factory in Crossgates, which had opened a year previously, there had been a huge explosion, which was one of Leeds's worst ever disasters.

On 5 December 1916, as some women were putting fuses to shells (which were packed with explosive) a huge explosion shook the whole place. There were thirty-eight deaths and a large number of injuries. But they were earning £12 a week, and the shells were urgently needed, so in spite of this horrific accident, the management had to move quickly and have the place up and running within a very short time.

Work was tough: shifts started at six in the morning and production never stopped, not even for public holidays; as one report has noted: 'The girls would inscribe cheeky messages on shells for the amusement

A group of workers at Barnbow shell factory. *Leeds Library*

of soldiers. … Working with TNT induced jaundice (earning them the nickname of 'canary girls') and other serious illnesses, including rotting teeth.'

Thanks to determined research by Ann Batchelor and others, we now know a lot more about the women who died at Barnbow. As Ann has pointed out, for wartime purposes of morale and reportage, publicity at the time was reduced. The factory was vast, extending over 400 acres,

and a special railway line was used to move the larger shells. Clearly this was dangerous work, as it involved working with fuses, and it appears that this explosion was caused by a poorly fixed fuse that had a spark alight on it.

There is now a list of those who died. The thirty-eight who died included James Thompson of Harrogate, who clung on to life until 31 May, and two Harrogate women, Ada Glassby and Emily Sedgewick.

There were heroic tales – notably that of William Parkin, who went into the place a dozen times to try to rescue people. Ann Batchelor has steadily gathered information, as has Carol Smithies, who, for instance, interviewed Sally Howe some years ago when she was a centenarian. Sally had worked at the factory as a teenager.

Even more than a year after the Barnbow explosion, there was still discussion of how much and for what reasons the munitions workers' demanding and dangerous conditions could be alleviated. *The Yorkshire Post*, on 7 August 1916, reported on a 'relay system': 'According to prominent labour leaders, who have been consulted, the interim report declares in favour of a brief period of rest for all munitions workers in certain conditions regarding length of service and good timekeeping.' One would have thought that the privations and risks involved in the work, and the frequency of life-threatening accidents, that there would have been more urgent reform.

This was one part in the huge, urgent national effort to produce munitions to feed the war. Historian Gerard de Groot has explained the source of this issue: 'Once stalemate descended upon the Western Front … heavy guns became transcendent. Only high-calibre, high explosive shells were even remotely effective against a heavily entrenched enemy.'

Munitions production was very dangerous work. There were toxic fumes to work with, and at any moment, a shell might explode. But the work had to be done, and it gave employment to almost a million women. There was, of course, the sorority of the job. One worker recalled, 'It was just magic; we worked and we stood and we sat and we sang. If anyone had come into the factory they never would have believed what had gone on.'

By August, when the accident was well behind any focus of attention, *The Yorkshire Post* carried an item that hints at perhaps one of many elements of reconsiderations regarding the workers. This was about the suggestion that munitions workers should have holidays on a relay system. The reporter comments, 'At the works the expectations are favourable to this matter, and the workers are grouped together in "fellowship" – each one of which is responsible for a particular branch of manufacture.' As usual, everything was based on teamwork and providing a sisterhood, a closeness in the working environment: from that basis, the relay system could be easily applied. Holidays were greatly needed, of course, when we bear in mind the nature of the work.

Chapter Four

1917: Tests of Courage

In reviewing the Leeds men who won VCs, some names are very slightly known, and we know very little of the details, but their discipline and achievement deserve to be better known, so some names are given here to mark this limited but important knowledge. One name, long before the Great War, was Edward McKenna, a colour sergeant in the 65th Regiment. He took command of thirty-five men and charged a much larger group of Maori warriors. As the enemy scattered and night came on, he had to hold his men tightly in silence all through the hours of darkness. It could be argued that to maintain that situation was harder than to have rashly charged or to have carried on firing – probably at shadows. That spirit and pluck is evident in the Leeds men who won the medal in the various theatres of war in 1914 to 1918.

Like Jack White, for instance. His commendation reads:

During an attempt to cross the Dialah River, Mesopotamia, he watched the two pontoons ahead of his raked by machine-gun fire. When his own pontoon was hit and every man beside him had been killed, he tied a telephone wire to the pontoon, dived overboard and towed it to shore.

A scene from the front, 1917. *Author's collection*

That was on 7–8 March 1917. He also saved the life of a wounded officer. Jack, born in Leeds, is actually buried in the Jewish Cemetery in Manchester.

The overarching narrative was, at first, the Germans' Operation Alberich, which entailed strengthening the Hindenburg Line of trenches. Then, between April and May there were battles, notably at Arras, and within that there was the notorious confrontation at Vimy Ridge. During that period, actually in early April, the United States entered the war.

At Arras, the Leeds Rifles, notably the 2nd/7th and the 2nd/8th Battalions, distinguished themselves, attacking a stretch of the long Hindenburg Line. They were also involved at Cambrai during this year, when the most intensive use of tanks marked the confrontation.

It was to be a year of remarkable courage. Among the people linked to awards and despatches there is one truly famous Leeds personality who came into prominence during these terrible years – Geoffrey Studdert Kennedy, known more widely as 'Woodbine Willie'. He was from an Irish family, his father having moved from Ireland to become vicar of St Mary's at Quarry Hill, Leeds. Religion was prominent in the family – Kennedy's grandfather had been Dean of Clonfert, in County Galway.

There were a number of Leeds curates who went off to join the Tommies. *The Yorkshire Post* used a photo of three of them, in their army chaplain uniforms: the Reverend H.L. Connor from St Matthews, Chapel Allerton; the Reverend L.S. Oliver (from Holy Trinity, Boar Lane); and the Reverend J. Duffield of St Clements, in Sheepscar. But it was Geoffrey Studdert Kennedy who stole the limelight.

Kennedy was born at the vicarage on 27 June 1893. One biographer described the area around Quarry Hill at the time: 'The area was dirty, a region of courts gas-lit, doubtful by night. There were those, indeed, who claimed Quarry Hill, Leeds, to be one of the worst slums in the North.' As Leeds readers will know, this was much later to be the site of the Quarry Hill Flats, built from 1935 to 1941, at the time thought to be an imaginative, aesthetically appealing project, slightly futuristic. It all went wrong, and they were eventually demolished in 1978. But in 1914, the Quarry Hill area and the Kennedy vicarage would have been at the very heart of Leeds, close to the Parish Church, the Calls and not far from the commercial and retail hub at Vicar Lane and the markets.

The local area was summed up by one writer neatly: 'brick kiln, Cemetery Tavern, Workhouse and all'. Kennedy senior, William Studdert Kennedy, died in the year the war began, and his wife, Joan, who had their nine children, died in 1913. William, the story goes, once

A portrait of Woodbine Willie in professional gear.

A sketch of Woodbine Willie.

put a hand on his son Geoffrey's head and said, 'His brain works so hard his head gets hot.' When the child was only two there was a storm, and a chimney at the vicarage was brought down. Amazingly, little Geoffrey was brought out unharmed.

Although he was a large, athletic man, he had suffered from asthma from the age of seven. His father said that Geoffrey had 'a horrid laugh', and there was, in spite of illness, a tough, outgoing man in the family, who was to make his mark in no uncertain terms. He was educated privately at first, but then went to the Leeds Grammar School, and later to the famous Trinity College, Dublin. One account of him at school in Leeds says a great deal about his character:

No one could mistake that upper lip; and if they did, the accent would have put them right. That was something he always tended to overdo. A fellow student at the Ripon Clergy School in after years exclaimed, 'I wish Kennedy wouldn't speak like a Dublin jarvie [coach driver] to show he's an Irishman!' But Kennedy did, and in times to come many thousands of people, including captains and kings of his day and age, heard him doing so, not always with approval.

One school friend at Leeds recalled, 'In temperament he was certainly older than most of us and I think his harmonizing influence was of great value.' This foreshadows the part he was to play in the war. In 1916, now a padre, he went out to Rouen in the thick of the war. Here he won his nickname of Woodbine Willie, walking down a train corridor to hand out cigarettes. This was as the train was about to take men up to the front from base. Kennedy wrote in a memoir:

> I begin at the top of the train and work down it, going into each carriage. I look round to their faces. I can always tell the man who has taken the trip before. You can see it in his eyes. … Often I have to cling on to finish the last carriages, creeping along the foot-board. At last, I am left alone looking after the disappearing tail-light. There is nothing glorious about this departure. It is all sordid and filthy. God only knows the hardships men endure on these journeys in packed and dirty carriages. No place to wash. No place to move, they sit and wait for eighteen hours or more until, I suppose they hear far off the sound of guns and know that the end is near.

Kennedy is most famous for his poems of the war, such as this, which was found, according to one biographer, on a piece of yellowed paper:

> *There's a Jerry over there, Sarge!*
> *Can't you see 'is big square 'ead?*
> *If 'e moves again I'll get 'im,*
> *Take these glasses 'ere and see.*
> *What's that? Got 'im through the 'ead Sarge?*
> *Where's my blarsted cup o' tea!*

It was at Messines Ridge that he won his Military Cross. He ran out into dangerous no-man's-land to try to help the wounded Tommies. This was in June, when the commander-in-chief, Haig, insisted on taking that ridge before the major fight known at the Third Battle of Ypres was to begin. If he had the Messines Ridge, the British would have the best lookout position for surveying a swathe of territory. On 7 June, the fight for the ridge began, and that meant detonating mines that the British had set. The artillery set about bombarding the place as well, and after that it was very slow progress for months, and heavy rain did not help at all.

In the midst of that was Woodbine Willie, risking his life to help others. He survived the war, and his published poetry was widely read. He wrote *Rough Rhymes of a Padre* (1918) and *More Rough Rhymes* (1919). The moment of heroism that won him the MC is described in the citation:

> For conspicuous gallantry and devotion to duty. He showed great courage and disregard for his own safety in attending to the wounded under heavy fire. He searched shell holes for our own and enemy, assisting them to the dressing station, and his cheerfulness and endurance had a splendid effect upon all ranks in the front line trenches, which he constantly visited.

Woodbine Willie was to become not merely a Leeds character, but a national figure – one of the great personalities of the war.

The war in the air was accelerating as well in early 1917. In the first years of the war, there had been a very high number of casualties sustained by the Royal Flying Corps (the precursor of the RAF) and flying had been more hazardous and risky to life than trench warfare, with a pilot having a frighteningly high chance of meeting death at the hands of a German machine gun fired from an enemy cockpit. The records of the war in the air contain a string of heroes, and many, such as Reginald Warneford, won high honours. He received the Victoria Cross for single-handedly destroying a Zeppelin. There were many more, all very young and brave.

We know a lot about the conditions of flying in the war, as a number of memoirs have come down to modern researchers. One piece of writing expresses the feeling well: 'On days when the clouds form almost a solid flooring, one feels very much at sea. ... Principally our work consists of keeping German airmen away from our lines, and in attacking them when opportunity offers.' Earlier in the war, before the technology of fixing machine guns that would fire through propellers, and before guns were more advanced, airmen would drop bombs by hand and fire guns at each other. It was primitive and extremely risky.

Towards the end of 1916 there had been an appeal for men to train as pilots and observers. There was a strong response to this, and the RFC found itself thoroughly reinforced and well up to strength by the spring of 1917. The pattern of recruitment is easy to discern. Men fighting on the ground would respond enthusiastically to something different, something to take them away from the mud and bombs. Of course they knew the high risks involved in flying, but there was the threat of imminent death everywhere, so this was the offer of a new adventure. On the website for Leeds WWI War Memorials (see bibliography) there are typical obituaries: some were pilots from the start and some were transferred. A typical second-wave, ex-army flyer was William Bowman, from Headingley, a lieutenant in the West Yorkshire Regiment. He gained a pilot's certificate at Ruislip, flying a Maurice Farman biplane. He was only twenty-two when he died in October 1916. On the other hand, Herbert Boyes was airman 2nd class, and nothing else. He died in March 1917.

We have a good idea of the danger involved in flying at the time from the letters of Harold Rosher, who flew the new Bebe, as did Bertram Wood (one of the most outstanding aces of the war in the air). He wrote, just before his death:

> The baby Nieuports are priceless. I flew one and went up the coast.
> … You have heard me mention Coulson … well he has just had an awfully bad crash at Dunkirk. Riley has also crashed badly twice out there. Ford too, is home on sick leave with his head cut open as a result of a bad crash and his passenger is not expected to live. If one goes flying long enough one is bound to get huffed [killed] in the end.

In June that year there was a meeting that put Leeds right in the centre of national news: the Leeds Convention, something described by

A scene from the war in the air. *Author's collection*

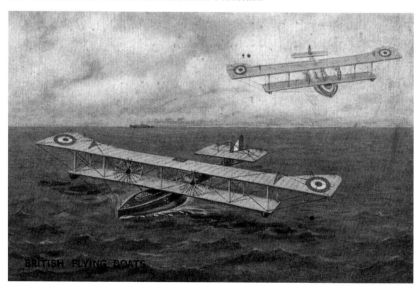

historian Ralph Miliband as 'perhaps the most remarkable gathering of the period'. This was to be a massive assembly of the various strands of the left in Britain, from the Independent Labour Party to the pacifists, and from the British Socialist Party to the union men. There were difficulties in finding a venue at first but eventually the Coliseum theatre on Cookridge Street was used. This had space enough for 3,400 people, and was normally used for variety shows and for circus production; it had been bought in 1901 by Taylors' Drug Company, and was later to be a cinema, complete with organ, ready to cater for the popularity of the black and white films that were all the rage just post-war.

The meeting was chaired by Robert Smillie, and there were to be a series of four resolutions: first, hailing Russia, where the Revolution had actually just happened; then a call for the establishment of international peace; the third one concerned civil liberties, embracing freedom of speech and a general amnesty for all political and religious prisoners; and finally, a call for councils in every town of workers' bodies.

Given that this was Britain, with both a comfortable Tory base and a rapid patriotism, such idealism was ambitious, to say the least, but events in Russia had galvanized the left into action. The importance of that revolution and the following murder of the Tsar and his family was best described by Ernest Bevin, long after the Leeds Conference:

Mrs Despard – one of the speakers at the 1917 Leeds meeting.
What Happened at Leeds pamphlet, 1917

Let us remember in 1951 that the Revolution of 1917 came to the working classes of Great Britain not as a social disaster, but as one of the most emancipating events in the history of mankind. ... Do not forget that in the early days when that great mass of backward people were trying to find their way to the light, they were trying to lift themselves from age-long penury and oppression, they were diverted from their objectives and thrown back into darkness, not by the malignancy of Stalin ... but by the action of Churchill, the City of London, New York and all the rest of the capitalist world.

It was quite an ordeal for the delegates. Constance Malleson, who was a war resister and friend of Bertrand Russell, gave an account of what it

✵ GLASGOW SELECT CHOIR. ✵

GRAND SCOTTISH CONCERT

IN AID OF THE LEEDS CHARITIES,

COLISEUM, LEEDS, Monday, November 29th, 1886.

PATRONS.

THE WORSHIPFUL THE MAYOR OF LEEDS (ALDERMAN GAUNT, J.P.).

RIGHT HON. SIR LYON PLAYFAIR, K.C.B. M.P.   SIR JAMES KITSON, BART.   SIR GEORGE MORRISON.
JOHN BARRAN, ESQ. M.P.   W. L. JACKSON, ESQ. M.P.   HERBERT J. GLADSTONE, ESQ. M.P.   G. W. BALFOUR, ESQ. M.P.
BRIGGS PRIESTLEY, ESQ. M.P.   ERNEST BECKETT, ESQ. M.P.   LAWRENCE GANE, ESQ. Q.C. M.P.
ARTHUR W. RUCKER, ESQ. F.R.S. &c.

CONCERT COMMITTEE AND GUARANTORS.

President:
JNO. C. MALCOLM, Esq.

Vice-Presidents:
JAMES DUNCAN, Esq.   P. M. R. BRODIE, Esq.

Honorary Secretaries:
ROBT. M. BURGESS.   ALEX. McLAUCHLAN.   THOS. EMMERSON.

Treasurer:
WM. A. M. BROWN, Esq.

JOHN BARR.	J. W. CURTIS.	DONALD McIVER.	D. ROBERTSON.
T. J. I. BLACKLOCK.	HECTOR DAVIDSON.	R. S. MACKENZIE.	JOHN V. ROGERS.
JAMES BURGESS.	ROBERT ELDER.	ALEX. MALTMAN.	GAVIN STEVENSON.
JOHN BURGESS.	DOUGLAS ELLIOT.	A. McCARMICK.	WM. TEBB.
P. E. CHUSNEY, JUN.	DAVID GIRVAN.	JOHN McGEORGE.	ROBERT WALLACE.
JAMES COLQUHOUN.	A. F. HOLROYD.	A. McKEAN.	JOHN WILLIAMSON.
WM. COLVILLE.	J. C. KERR.	D. J. MILLER.	WM. WILSON.
JOHN CRAIG.	WM. LYALL.	FRED. RHODES.	J. W. WOOTTON.

✵ PROGRAMME. ✵

Part First

GLEE	"Strike the Lyre"	Coote.
PART SONG	"Afton Water"	Arr. by Patterson.
SONG	"Behold Love Song"	Pinsuti.
HUMOROUS PART SONG	"Last May a braw wooer"	Arr. by Archer.
BALLADS	"Soldiers brave and gallant be"	Gastoldi.
DUET	"Row weel, my Boatie"	R. A. Smith.
PART SONG	"The Rowan Tree"	Arr. by Allan.
HUMOROUS PART SONG	"Three Doughtie Men"	Pearson.
SONG	"I lo'e na a Laddie but ane"	(Burns)
PART SONG	"Scots wha ha'e"	Arr. by Patterson.

Part Second

PART SONG	"Corn Rigs"	Arr. by Archer.
PART SONG	"Evening"	Leslie.
SONG	"I gaed a waefu' gate yestr'en"	(Burns)
HUMOROUS PART SONG	"Kate Dalrymple"	Archer.
PART SONG	"The Bells"	Lahee.
SONG	"O for the Rowes o' my ain native Heather"	Glover.
HUMOROUS PART SONG	"The Wedding of Shon McLean"	Patterson.
PART SONG	"Hey! Ca' thro'"	Arr. by Moodie.
TRIO	"The Laughing Gipsies"	Glover.
PART SONG	"The Garb of Old Gaul"	Arr. by Patterson.
	"Auld Lang Syne."	

Conductor   -   Mr. J. Millar Craig.

A programme for the Coliseum; the building was later used for the great Socialist meeting in 1917. *Author's collection*

was like in the city as they were abused by the crowd: 'The crowd hissed as we went through the streets … some of the children threw stones. There were a lot of people about.' The hotels had refused to receive the delegates and the arriving visitors had to rely on friends to tell them where friendly leftist characters could be found to give them shelter.

The writer for the *Daily Herald*, who compiled a long report, noted what was in the minds of the activists at the time: 'The drive to find cannon-fodder from the factories, coupled with the intensification of dilution, was producing a veritable explosion of feeling among the skilled trade unionists ... who found themselves working for wages considerably lower than the earnings of semi-skilled and unskilled workers who were able to benefit from piecework.'

The same author ended his report with a flat statement of disappointment: 'The fate of the convention, its lapse from the status of central importance ... to a mere episode among the footnotes of Labour history, is part of the history of a long succession of defeats which the Labour movement encountered.'

There was something else that happened after the convention, and it is a stigma on the city. There were violent incidents in the streets based on anti-Semitic feeling. David Thornton, in an account of Leeds in the war, notes that 'Leeds had a reputation for anti-Semitism' and indeed, my own experience growing up in the city in the 1950s, confirms that. The reasons are not easy to identify. It was based, as always, on fear and bigotry. Thornton points out that in 1917 the trouble was partly the result of provocation by miners and older men who incited younger men to violence. It explains why there were so many features in the Leeds papers trying very hard to give the Jewish citizens a good, positive patriotic image. The fights and attacks only stopped when the police came out in force. It was a black mark, and a sad contrast to the optimism of the leftist speakers and thinkers who had filled the Coliseum.

Shortages were kicking in this year. Every conceivable measure was being taken to grow food and to conserve it. Domestic economy was the watchword. The mayor at this time, Lupton, summarized in his memoir the situation regarding shortages and other plans put in place. He notes that the Ministry of Food restrictions had an effect and that 'a hurried visit had to be made to headquarters and permits for the release of greater quantities had to be demanded.' He had some problems in using his position and power to achieve this, and he points out that, as with the Second World War, growing your own was the key: 'Owing to the food scarcity, the allotment movement, which had commenced in the previous year, grew enormously. Many fields and such pieces of waste land as were suitable were taken for the purpose all over the city, the most noticeable example being Woodhouse Moor, upon which hundreds of allotments developed.'

This did seem to have a very positive effect. He adds, 'To grow one's own vegetables and to realize their superiority to any that could be bought was a revelation to many, and terrible as the war was, yet one of the good things that came out of it has been the growth of the allotment movement.'

But shortages always bring a number of spin-off problems. As David Thornton, the historian, has noted, in late 1917 and early 1918, 'Panic buying over food brought the prospect of rationing nearer. By the last week of December 1917, Leeds Cattle Market had only fourteen beef cattle on sale.' He points out that some areas devised their own rationing schemes. The one commodity that everyone recalling shortages mentions was sugar. In many areas, children and teachers were making special efforts to save for sugar, and even, at times, the teachers were employed filling sugar bags. But rationing and shortages provoked all kinds of advice, some of it in verse, as in these lines from Aelfrida Tillyard:

A slice of swede is what you need,
And please don't leave the peel.
But there's dessert for you, my love,
Some glucose stewed with sloes.
And now good night – your dreams be bright!
(Perhaps they will – who knows?)

Propaganda brings publications, of course, and the *Win-the-War Cookery Book* was ideal for domestic economy and all its strictures. Other evocative titles were *Housekeeping on Twenty-Five Shillings a Week,* and for the wealthier citizens, *Patriotic Food Economy for the Well-to-Do.*

The year ended with at least the tiniest inkling of some radical change in the trajectory of the war: on 16 December, Russia arranged an armistice with the Central Powers. But in the near future, this was not good news for the Allies, because the German forces on the Eastern Front could now be transported to the West – exactly what had been envisaged by the Schlieffen Plan at the beginning of the war.

Chapter Five

1918: The Final Battles and the End

For so many, the beginning of another year could only have meant more of the same: draw in the breath, tighten the belt, grin and bear it – for Yorkshire folk the old response to a greeting of 'Mustn't grumble' became almost a national exhortation.

In the spring of the year, the German offensive began, and it has become known as the Kaiser's Battle, or Operation Michael. There was a massive advance on the British Third and Fifth armies. This almost achieved a wedge between the British and French armies, with a tactic known as 'infiltration' – an intense use of manpower in a circumscribed location. The Germans were, in fact, only around 60 miles from Paris at the time. It was possible to fire the huge guns at the city, and the Germans brought in some of their Krupp guns, which were carried in rail wagons.

It was a truly huge army, which advanced in May: General Max von Boehn was in command, with the Seventh Army, and the First Army had Bruno von Mudra in charge. Their joint force amounted to forty-

A card sent home from France in 1918. *Author's collection*

four divisions, and they were opposed by the French Sixth Army, with three British divisions in support.

The German front line extended from the sea south of Ostend, right down to the Aisne, to the east of Rheims. At Lys, in April, the Allied front lines were defended by several Commonwealth forces, including Australian, New Zealand and South African men. This action was defined in part by the terrible use of poison gas by the Germans.

Ludendorff was in command, and facing him for the Allies were Marshall Foch, for the French, and General Gough, commanding the Fifth Army. Ludendorff had promised the Reichstag that the offensive would be a great success, in spite of the certainty of a high number of losses. The aim was to isolate the British, and the chief strategic tool was the German railway system, which, from behind the lines, could rush troops to any desired location very smartly.

The Germans crossed the canal at Oise, and the hard fact for the British was that their fourteen divisions were to encounter forty German divisions. They carried all before them at first, but as one historian puts it, they lost momentum by 27 March: 'the great vigour of the attack had exhausted the attacking armies, their communications now lay across the devastated area and rain was hampering their movements.' On the 28th, they moved forward, but were frustrated and it was a desperate impasse.

It was in April that George Sanders, the VC winner whose tale was told in Chapter 3, was with his West Yorks regiment at Mount Kemmel. Once again, Sanders was an outstandingly brave soldier. He was taken prisoner and had serious wounds both to right arm and right leg, and the last sighting anyone had of him was with him still moving around, gun in hand. Actually, he was taken prisoner, to Limburg Camp. But in the ruck, his conduct won him the Military Cross. The place where he won the award, Mount Kemmel, had been heavily shelled by the Germans, and then they had surrounded the French and British forces who were there. There was desperate hand-to-hand combat, and after the German triumph, it was claimed that 6,000 Allied prisoners had been taken. There was even one note that said that the Kaiser himself watched the battle.

As hostilities began in Europe in the new year, the most obvious addition to the conflict was the American army. Thousands of new fighters were now standing alongside the Allied powers. The great offensive, 'Michael', was going to be, in the words of the time, 'a big show'. The men of the Leeds Pals were now joined by men from other battalions, and

Ypres
Yper
Ypres
Menin. Mémorial des Héros Britanniques.
'oort. Gedenkteeken der Britische Helden.
n Gate. Memorial of British Heroes.

The Menin Gate – the famous memorial in the heart of the Western Front. *Author's collection*

by the end of February there had been a grand reshuffle, so that, as Laurie Milner summarizes, the 31st Division was now a hotchpotch of various groups, with the Pals as 15th/17th West Yorkshire Regiment. At the end of March, the Leeds men were to move in to relieve the 11th Suffolks. Such was the enemy onslaught that a gradual falling back was ordered, and the whole force of the 93rd Brigade was facing a renewed German attack, followed by more, and an unexplained incident left a gap that cut off the Pals. There was nothing for it but for the Pals to stay put and hold. It was at this time that Sergeant Albert Mountain won his VC.

The situation in which he won the award was that a massive German attack was launched, and the retention of a strategically important ridge was a priority. Mountain was the man for the job. Laurie Milner explains what happened:

Sergeant Mountain … volunteered, and, with ten men and a Lewis gun, succeeded in enfilading the German advance patrol, killing about a hundred – the remainder fled. The main body of the enemy then appeared and Mountain and his men formed a defensive position in order to cover the retirement of his company, although by this time, there were only four of the ten men left.

Mountain, from Garforth, was only twenty-two years old. He lived through the next war as well, dying in 1967. The important section of his official citations reads:

> For most conspicuous bravery and devotion to duty during an enemy attack, when his company was in an exposed position on a sunken road, having hastily dug themselves in. Owing to the intense artillery fire, they were obliged to vacate the road and fall back. The enemy meantime was advancing en masse, preceded by an advanced patrol about 200 strong. The situation was critical and volunteers for a counter-attack were called for. Sergeant Mountain immediately stepped forward, and his party of ten men followed him. He then advanced on the flank with a Lewis gun and brought enfilade to bear. … At this time the main body appeared and the men, who were numerically many times weaker than the enemy, began to waver. Sergeant Mountain rallied and organized his party and formed a defensive position. …With this party of one non-commissioned officer and four men, he successfully held at bay 600 of the enemy for half an hour.

There were prisoners taken, and the continued threat of snipers.

What was this terrible flu? People were familiar with it, because there had been outbreaks in recent times – in 1900, 1908, and even in 1915, when health and strength were particularly in demand. It was a horrible ravager of life and well-being, with its warning signs of sweating, headaches and pains along the back and in the eyes. Even worse, it sent the victim's mood down low, into depression and world-weariness. Now, in 1918, it was percolating through the ranks of the young men returning home from the trenches. Then it incubated in all kinds of places, from picture houses to markets, wherever crowds gathered.

To make matters worse, there was an acute shortage of medical professionals, from nurses up to doctors. The health advisers who were available, at the very top, from whence advice was sought, could offer nothing except the efficacy of alcohol and sleep. The flu took its victims in an agonizing manner, basically filling their lungs and full respiratory system with liquid – some of this being the person's own blood – and effectively drowning them. Desperation set in as well. As Juliet

Typical fringe medicine cures at the time of the flu. *Author's collection*

Nicolson, author of a study of post-1918 Britain, pointed out, 'Older people were accustomed to warding off illness and used their own remedies. Opium, rhubarb, treacle, laudanum, vinegar and quinine were all thought to have their own special curative powers.'

It was a reign of terror that summer. Children had a rhyme:

I had a little bird
Its name was Enza.
I opened the window
And in flew Enza.

The horrendous disease spread everywhere, and of course it was ravaging the servicemen. In a chat group on the website Great War Forum/Armed Forces of the Great War (see bibliography) there was a discussion in 2008 on this subject. One contributor wrote that an account he had found was 'the most harrowing I have ever read'. This was the passage, which was originally in the *Harrogate Herald*:

Photo by   *Yeι*

The Hon. LADY DOROTHY WOOI Commandant, Templenewsam V.A. Hospital.

Some of the commandants who kept th hospitals organized and regulated. *Leeds*

The funeral of Private Harry Hainsworth of the Leeds Pals (15th West Yorks.), son of Mr and Mrs J. Hainsworth of 109, Dragon Parade, Harrogate, who died from pneumonia following influenza on November 29th at Roundhay Road Military Hospital, Leeds, took place at Grove Road Cemetery on Wednesday last. The deceased was accorded a military funeral, which was largely attended. Military mourners were present from his own regiment, and the firing party and bearers were from the Honourable Artillery Company from Leeds. The coffin was covered with the Union Jack, and the service was conducted by Rev D.S.Guy MA, vicar of Christ Church. The 'Last Post' was sounded at the graveside. The family and friends were present at the funeral with the exception

Miss E. S. Innes, R.R.C.,
on-in-Chief, 2nd Northern General
Hospital.

Photo by   *Hartnell.*

Miss E. M. Cliff, O.B.E.,
Commandant, Gledhow Hall V.A.D.
Hospital.

of Mr Hainsworth, who was at the bedside of another son, Lieu
Geo Hainsworth, who passed away from the same malady the same
evening.

Of course, many men went through the hell of trench warfare only to be
infected by the flu. Private Leonard Smith of the Leeds Pals, for instance,
from Farnley, served in Egypt, and then at the Somme on the opening
day of the assault. He suffered from severe shrapnel wounds, and then
was taken to a dressing station before going to hospital in Calais. He
then returned to the fighting, attached to the Royal Engineers. We might
think that such a man deserved a break when it came to the great
pandemic of influenza, but in November 1918 he caught the infection.

But luck was on his side: he survived, after treatment at Chapel Allerton, then was married and had four children. He lived until 1958.

They are not all tragic stories. But the disease did not disappear overnight. In October there was a recurrence: the papers reported that, in mid-October, there had been 1,895 influenza deaths in one week. Yorkshire was severely affected, with seventy-one deaths in Hull in that week, sixty-nine in Sheffield and thirty-nine in Leeds.

At home in Leeds, we have the sad statistics of what was a pandemic: truly awesome proportions of infection. In one week in October, there were 4,482 deaths in ninety-six towns that *The Times* selected for a representative study of flu-related deaths. In the first week of November, one report about Leeds gave the figure of just over 200 deaths between mid-January and early February. The national death rate was fifty-one per thousand. Eventually, by the end of November, there was a perceived decline in the number of fatalities. One figure of 1,644 for the country as a whole, on 21 November, is, in spite of the high figure, a slowing down.

There is a note of frustration and tiredness, regarding the summer of 1918, even in the post-war histories. Scott's monumental Leeds chronicle, for instance, points out that resources were still being drained to the dregs, as it were, with all available cadres of men (and boys) being attuned to war. He notes:

> As the summer of 1918 wore on, with its continual calls to economy … special duties were again found for our schoolboys. For example, in July, volunteers to do harvesting work in Cumberland were asked for; and the Grammar School, Boys' Modern School, Cockburn High School and West Leeds High School all sent their quota of boys who received 3d an hour for their labour.

The Boy Scouts did their bit as well. In August, Mr Wheeler, commissioner of the local Boy Scouts Association, had 600 Boy Scouts out at Bramham to pull flax. It was all part of a great chain of production, because the flax was needed for linen manufacture, and the linen was used for the making of aircraft wings. This was far from trivial. The government, from the first week of the year, had revived flax production on a large scale. The Board of Agriculture made it clear that in some areas, farmers would be told to grow flax and other crops, rather than food crops. The Russian ports had been closed, and so imports were less abundant; the rate of loss for the planes over the battlefields was very high. Flax was therefore in high demand, and in the spring of 1918, 10,000 acres were planted. The Board circulated the basic facts:

> Flax-growing was at one time very extensively practised in this country and it is understood that new centres will be in districts where it flourished in the past, viz: Yorkshire, Lincolnshire, Fife and Somerset. A nucleus for the new industry already exists in Yeovil, at Somerset and at Selby in Yorkshire. At these places the British Flax and Hemp Growers Society and the University of Leeds respectively have carried on both the growing of the crop and the conversion of the straw into fibre with marked success for several years.

As was always the case in dire need, everything had been worked out; farmers growing flax were to receive £8 10s per ton of seed and straw. The government even guaranteed a payment of £14 per acre for anyone trying the flax-growing for the first time, and who would be lacking experience.

The early months of 1918, as W.H. Scott recalls, were showing the very down-hearted atmosphere resulting from shortages, suffering and sheer war-weariness. He explains this sense of limbo in this way: 'But neither the fuel control nor the curfew weighed the scale of fortune down as depressingly as the "last straw" – the ever-present reminder of what our men were enduring at the front checked any tendency to murmur at our home circumstances.' He quotes an anonymous passage on a 'night scene' in Leeds at that time:

> After 10.30 when the theatres discharge their bustling crowds, Briggate and Boar Lane, except at the weekend, are empty. Not quite though. The trams are there, and lively munitions girls, laughing and chatting, climb into them with their little sandwich cases, and are soon whisked off home. At 11 o'clock the streets are deserted, and the trams have only an odd passenger or two.

There was still an attempt by the government to conscript yet more men. Early in the year there was widening of the net, and even an attempt to introduce conscription in Ireland, but that had failed. There had been another Military Service Act, and the second wave of conscription. The fact is that the government was aware that there was an approaching crisis with regard to the overall military resources needed to continue the war. Looking across the condition of the forces on active service, it would have been a simple matter to see that morale was at a low ebb. The war was a war of attrition with heavy losses; technological warfare and biological warfare had been introduced, and now there was an increasing problem of the welfare of the men.

We could add to this, now that research into a most outrageous element of the Great War has been undertaken, the incidence of death sentences passed and executed on servicemen. Anthony Babington has looked into this subject thoroughly, and he gives several instances of such death sentences. In 1916, at the height of this tense and worrying situation for the top brass, when morale and determination were paramount in all cases, Babington has shown that there were ninety-five executions in the British Army: ninety-three in France and Belgium, one in Gallipoli and one in German East Africa. Babington makes the point that, when men were urgently needed, corners were cut. He quotes words from a committee that had been set up to study shell shock: 'Many recruits were passed into the army,' they said, 'who were quite unfit to withstand the rigours of a campaign or even, in many cases, preparatory training.' As the *Sunday Independent* featured in May 1992, 'After the war, the Army Council set up a committee to examine the executions, but its report was never published.'

There was also the universal problem faced by the male population: if they were not actually aged or crippled, the 'white feather' mentality and the pervading sense of shame went on. In one provincial newspaper there was a classic example of the kind of social issue that tended to appear in this situation: it was a matter of who had or had not attested for enlistment under the Derby Scheme:

> In Leeds, the proportion of married men to single men who have attested is as two to one, and not many more than half the single men have come forward. Of those single men who have attested, it is computed that at least 50 per cent did so in the hope that they would be relieved from service as men engaged in reserved occupations. ... Thus, out of the several thousands of Leeds young men who are in the four groups called up for service next month, more than half of the number have appealed to the local tribunal for exemption.

When these men had signed their short service attestation form, the small print had read:

> Oath to be taken on attestation ... I will be faithful and bear true allegiance to His Majesty King George the Fifth, his heirs and successors, and that I will, as in duty bound, honestly and faithfully defend His Majesty, his heirs and successors, in Person, Crown

An attestation certificate for Wybert Birtle. *Courtesy Martin Birtle*

Lieut.-Col. STUART C. TAYLOR,
15th Battalion West Yorkshire Regiment
(Leeds " Pals ").

Capt. L. BATHURST (R.A.M.C.),
15th Battalion West Yorkshire Regi
(Leeds " Pals ").

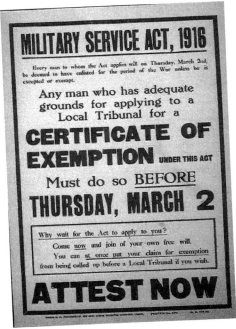

A poster relating to conscription.

A group of the leading lights in military Lee
Leeds Library

and Dignity against all enemies and I will serve and obey all orders.

They had also signed for the duration of the war and also to agree to these words: 'If employed with hospitals, depots of mounted units or as a clerk etc., you may be retained after the termination of hostilities until your service can be spared, but such retention shall in no case exceed six months.'

On 23 March 1918, the War Cabinet had their meeting. It was held in a state of emergency, and the worrying topic

to by   *Bacon & Son.*
Lieut.-Col. J. W. STEAD, V.D.,
Battalion West Yorkshire Regiment
(Leeds " Pals ").

Photo by   *Bacon & Son.*
Lieut.-Col. E. KITSON CLARK, T.D.,
8th Battalion West Yorkshire Regiment
(Leeds Rifles).

of the day was the manpower problem. There were men standing by –
5,000 officer cadets and 88,000 infantry on leave, for instance – but on
the other hand there had been immense losses in the theatre of war in
Europe. Over the previous two years, the government had failed to
coerce the objectors, and the tribunals, with their exemptions, had
proved to be a constant headache for the hard-pressed field command,
always wanting more men. Temporary exemptions, which were a way
out of tricky ethical problems for the benches running the tribunals, had
been a common occurrence, and that again slowed down the process of
gathering fresh men for service, coerced or otherwise.

There was also the issue of the government promise of not sending
teenagers out to the front – at least, not 18-year-olds. But even in those
early months, it was clear to the High Command and to the politicians

that the human resources were insufficient to give them confidence if the struggles ahead proved to be as demanding as they were deemed to be. In that meeting in March, the pledge concerning 18-year-olds was erased. That showed utter desperation. The statement given was simply that the emergency that had always been expected 'had arisen'. The man who had the unenviable task of boosting manpower was Sir Eric Geddes, at that time the First Lord of the Admiralty. The other members looked to Geddes to come up with some ideas about raising men to fight. He it was who advocated raising the age limit, and he claimed that he could raise 300,000 men that way. But then came the topic of Ireland, and Viscount French, who was in command of the forces at home, considered that Ireland would be fertile ground for recruitment. Geddes had seemed impressive when he had said that he proposed 'to increase the total amount of manpower available and to remove obstacles which stand in the way of full mobilization of our manpower and for tapping such new sources as still remain'.

A few days after that meeting, Lloyd George spoke with the Chief Secretary of the War Cabinet, H.E. Duke, and then to General Byrne of the Royal Irish Constabulary, and Lloyd George's response to Byrne's opinion was summarized by historian Ken Coates:

> By passing and enforcing such a measure, both the whole of the Catholics and nationalists in Ireland would be united against the British Empire. ... He claimed that there would be the greatest difficulty enlisting men, that there would be riots, and he was very doubtful what the worth of the recruits would be.

In May, Herbert Samuel, the former Home Secretary, came to speak on the subject of conscription to the Yorkshire Liberal Association in Leeds. He lamented that there was no magnanimity to be expected of Irishmen in respect of fighting for England. He dismissed any idealistic thoughts in that quarter; he took advantage of the occasion to speak about Germany, and his words must have hit home very emotionally in West Yorkshire, as there had been so much German settlement there throughout the previous century:

> He was a member of the Cabinet for five years before the war and he had no reason to be ashamed of the fact that during all that period they honestly sought friendly relations with Germany. Seldom had the action of statesmen been so vindicated as had been the policy of Mr Asquith and Viscount Grey by the Lichnowsky revelations.

Whippet tanks in action. *Author's collection*

Lichnowsky was a German diplomat who had tried to avert war, working to persuade Germany not to be drawn into supporting Serbia and starting the horrendous repercussions leading to Britain and Germany facing each other.

The funds raised by the Tank Weeks grew apace. At the beginning of this year, contributions to the Tank funds in Birmingham alone had reached £1.5 million. In the north, *The Yorkshire Observer* published a special edition, when the Tank Bank reached Bradford, and that city's total in January was £3 million. That was surely a challenge, given the Leeds and Bradford rivalry, though no figures are available. But the national effort was huge, and one report typifies the urgency of the fund-raising:

> … before Christmas, of the whole amount subscribed for National War Bonds and War Savings Certificates from all sources throughout the country more than one third was paid through the four Tank Banks at Bristol, Leeds, Manchester and Portsmouth. It is necessary to make a sum of £25,000 each week by the sales of National War Bonds. This represents roughly an average of 10s per head of the population per week – man, woman and child.

At the end of May, the King paid a visit to Leeds. He had toured the West Riding and spent time at textile works, and had generally been a presence. *The Times* focused on the King and Queen and the clothing industry:

This morning in visits to clothing factories in Leeds, they were shown how standard suits for civilians were turned out. With the increasing scarcity of cloth for ordinary purposes the possibility of a very general adoption of standard clothes has to be considered. Should the suits become the only method of clothing the nation, those who study fashion will probably make a note of the fact that the King today gave an order for a mixture of brown cloth which, in a ready-made style, can be sold at £2 17s 6d. Their Majesties saw a wide range of standard clothing at the establishment of Messrs David Little and Co.

Clearly, this was an anticipation of what would be around after the Second World War – Utility clothes for everyone.

Of course, the royal party went to Leeds Town Hall, the venue for all really grand occasions. The press report assured the readers that, 'The King must have returned to London convinced of the downright loyalty of the West Riding.' Someone had worked out some staggering statistic, in a world without computers: 'It is estimated that in three days he has heard the cheers of a million men, women and children.'

In July, there was an ammunitions dispute, and other industrial troubles. At a Leeds conference, representing 300,000 munitions workers, a general strike was called. There was some opposition from its own ranks: some wanted a return to work as long as a committee of enquiry was created. At the same time, the National Engineering and Allied Trades Council had their conference in Leeds. All this farrago of heated discussions and petulance had one cause – an embargo. This was something that had escalated from a problem at first located at the Daimler company: they were employing too many skilled workers. The government placed an embargo on this recruitment, and that then spread to other places.

There were deeper union problems though, as union leader Dudley Docker wrote in a report: 'Many workers ... no longer place the reliance they formerly did on their union leaders but are inclined to break away from any bargain on small provocation.'

Then, at last, the war was over. The Armistice was one of those rare occasions at which there was general rejoicing and very little trouble in the streets. W.H. Scott, described the scene in and around the Town Hall and Victoria Square. The Town Hall and the Art Gallery had been focal points for so much that had been crucially important for the city in the war years. Now, as Scott recalled, the current mayor, Joseph Henry, took centre stage:

Part of the procession for the royal visit to Leeds in 1918.
Author's collection

… he appeared on the steps of the Town Hall to address the many thousands who assembled in the Square and its approaches. It was estimated that fully 40,000 people were present. With the Police Band playing exhilarating national music, and the youngsters in the throng singing *When the boys come home*, the effect on everyone was electric. Then, when night came, there were fireworks and bonfires, for the ban in respect of these was promptly withdrawn … the streets were full of animated, good-humoured throngs bubbling over with excitement and yet causing no disorder.

The peace had not been straightforward. There had been a gradual cessation of hostilities, with those at the Eastern Front ending at the end of the previous year. But the one that really counted was actually agreed and signed at that now iconic time of 5.00 am on 11 November. There had been discussions during the previous week, and at the heart of the negotiations were the fourteen points put forward by President Woodrow

Wilson. Consequently came the momentous meeting in the railway carriage belonging to the French general, Foch, and as far as Germany was concerned, its first task was to evacuate the Western Front. As always happens, a neutral zone was created while the winding down was in progress.

There were those who, when peace was imminent, wanted blood and revenge in the most heartless way possible. One Leeds businessman, of the Castleton Foundry in Armley, wrote to *The Times* to make the extreme position very clear, and he thought that most British folk shared his views:

> The reasoned opinion of 99 per cent of the people of this country is emphatically the unconditional surrender of Germany and the infliction upon the arch-criminal of the world's history of the most onerous, humiliating and disastrous terms possible short of extermination. President Wilson's fourteen points of last January must be cancelled. They were refused with contempt by the Germans at a time when they expected to end the war victoriously; so why should we now feel bound by them, much water having run under London Bridge since that time?

After the celebrations, Leeds, along with every town and city in the land, turned its thoughts to rebuilding – in every sense. The council was soon in planning mode, thinking about the urgent need for housing and jobs.

Chapter Six

1919:The Aftermath

The shock waves after a war finally ends are immeasurable. They extend across society, visible in the public words and speeches, and in the rhetoric in the press. But they also extend inside, deep into the hearts and souls of those who have survived and endured. In 1919 there was the generation who had not only endured the shortages and the fear, the resolve to be strong and the refusal to accept the inevitable losses and scarcities, these were people who had also waited for the telegrams, informing them that a loved-one had died, was missing or was severely wounded. This was a generation who had had to learn to put on a brave face, to show the stiff upper lip expected of the British. Now they were asked to consider memorials.

These memorials took many forms too, though the notion of civic and public memorials took pride of place. In one respect at least, with

One of the memorials to the war outside the Art Gallery. *Author's collection*

this in mind, Leeds was at the forefront. This was the founding of the British War Graves Association, the brainchild of Sarah Ann Smith, from Stourton. She had lost her son at Arras, where he was buried.

Noel Reeve, writing on Smith for the Leeds University website, makes the point that Smith was at the heart of a debate over whether or not it was possible to bring home more of the bodies of the dead, rather than simply bury them close to where they had fallen. A letter in the *Yorkshire Evening News* in May had expressed what many were feeling:

> Now the government has decided to remove the bodies of the fallen from the scattered cemeteries to large central cemeteries, why cannot they allow relatives who so desire to have them brought home to be placed in a family grave? Nurse Cavell's body is being brought over to England, and why not others? I think the feeling is very strong against this attitude of the government, who claimed our boys when living, and now they have sacrificed their lives we are to be robbed of their dear remains which belong to us and are ours alone.

There was a large-scale meeting in Leeds debating the topic, and Mrs Smith played a part in creating a petition. At a YMCA meeting, a letter was read from the American President, and any financial objection was challenged. A series of letters were then written and published in the local press, examining the repercussions of such removals. The main objection was brutally honest and explicit, expressed in one letter, 'Would it be wise to bring these bodies here? Think what it would mean to take up bodies who have died in full flesh and have lain for a long time.' But Mrs Smith put the argument for the return of bodies in highly emotional terms: 'This garment clothed our loved ones, who we have watched and cared for since childhood. Now we cry out to have this beloved body restored to us. It is our very own and we would wish to have it buried with due reverence and tend its grave with our own hands.'

The plan did not work out, but it was significant. Noel Reeve summed up what was

The general war memorial by the Art Gallery. *Author's collection*

at least a second-choice measure: 'They did, however, organize and assist many people to visit the graves of the fallen at Whitsuntide every year. Mrs Smith missed only one year until her death in 1936.'

As Gill Thomas has noted, 'More than 6 million men went away to war. This was 28 per cent of the male population. An enormous number of these men were wounded (1,676,037); some of them were disabled for life. Nearly all women knew someone who fought in the war and who was maimed or killed.' Vera Brittain, author of the classic work *Testament of Youth*, wrote, 'On every side there seemed to be despair and no way out. … Every thought brought nothing but darkness and pain.'

Another memoir, by Methodist minister J. Barlow Brooks, describes the post-war trauma very strongly:

> Returned prisoners from Germany – stretcher-cases from hospitals – crippled men and others who had come through without a scratch – we did our best to give them all a warm welcome home. Their stories were varied and their explanations as to how they came through it all were just as varied. There were pagan as well as fatalistic reasons as well as more religious ones. Some said bluntly that their names had not been on any of the bombs or bullets that came their way.

In short, peace had been longed for, and by so many, but when it arrived, it was another variety of shock, for it brought other questions, more demands and, most of all, a sudden hiatus in which there had to be an acknowledgement of the need for mourning, before the mourning itself was given a space in life.

But there was one heartening local story: that of Private Lonsdale, referred to in Chapter 2. This was the Leeds tram conductor who had been sentenced to death for striking a German officer while a prisoner of war. The press announced, just as the new year began, that he was 'expected in Leeds today … he says his weight dropped from 11 stones and a half to seven stones, and then he was put on double rations. He is believed to be the only prisoner in Germany so treated. He is preparing to return to his work on the trams.' It must have been a cheery scrap of news in such depressing times.

When, finally, the return of peace was certain, in the midst of all the celebrations and rituals, there was one particularly Yorkshire-centred announcement in the press that signalled that normality was resumed in at least one important respect – in the world of cricket. There had been rather revolutionary suggestions made about experiments and trials of newfangled games. At the annual meeting of the Yorkshire Cricket Club, Lord Hawke said that the championship was impossible unless matches were played in equal conditions. The gentlemanly statement was made:

> Yorkshire would stand by the counties who wished to give two-day cricket a fair trial. As to Saturday starts, Lord Hawke said they were not supported at the meeting of the Advisory Committee, as expense must be considered. Finally, Lord Hawke said that for the coming season, Yorkshire would have the services of Hirst, Rhodes, Denton, Kilner, Drake and Dolphin, and also many young players. Lord Hawke was re-elected President.

Those names were stars indeed: George Hirst and Wilfred Rhodes were formidable. Cricket historian Michael Brearley sums up their status at the time: 'No other county but Yorkshire has ever had as contemporaries two such prolific all-rounders as Hirst and Wilfred Rhodes. Although Rhodes was six years the younger, they played together over 400 times in the same Yorkshire side.' In the last season before the war began, Rhodes had scored 1,377 runs.

There had been disruption to cricket, of course, through the war, as there was to all sport. But, cricket being the closest thing to a county religion in Yorkshire, there had been grievous losses of talented players. Major Booth, for instance, had died at the Somme. William Booth, born in Pudsey in 1886, played for the county from 1908 to 1914, and in the latter year he was named as one of the Wisden Cricketers of the Year. He took a commission in the West Yorkshire Regiment, in which he was a second lieutenant. He was one of the casualties of the very first day of the Somme, having been commissioned a year before that fateful day. His regiment was the Leeds Pals, and along with him was fellow cricketer Abe Waddington. This is one of the most poignant stories of the war as far as Leeds was concerned, as Abe stayed with Booth, and as the obituary has it, he stayed with him until he died. The team lost a superb right-hand batsman and a true gentleman soldier.

Cricket has been a metaphor for imperial war, of course, for a very long time, perhaps most familiar in Sir Henry Newbolt's poem *Vitae Lampada*, with its celebrated line, in the midst of battle, of *'Play up! Play up and play the game!'* But, as Tom Rowley makes clear in a feature article about cricket in the war, 'Across the country, cricketers were changing out of their whites and into uniform.' He points out that of 278 professional cricketers in England that summer (1914), 210 signed up to fight.

In a book by Christopher Sandford, *The Final Over*, details of some of the diaries of these men have emerged to be read. Arguably the greatest batsman of them all, W.G. Grace, wrote, 'The time has arrived when the county cricket season should be closed. … It is not fitting at a time like this that able-bodied men should be playing day after day, and pleasure seekers look on.' Tom Rowley notes that, 'Many heeded the call. Matches were abruptly cancelled while one county side missed victory by five runs when their captain was called up.'

In March, the influenza struck again. In the period from February to March there were over 200 deaths in Leeds from the infection. But it was a worldwide phenomenon. In India, 4 per cent of the people had been victims; in the USA, far more died of the flu than had perished in the war. Juliet Nicolson, in her history of British society immediately post-war, explains a deeper consequence of this suffering, after so much had been endured already: 'People felt that the Church, and by association, God, had let them down. During the course of the preceding five years, when every family in the land had known suffering, pain and death, our churches even in remote villages became recruiting agencies, our pulpits were used as political booths.' In an oral history project undertaken in Leeds in the 1970s, one respondent told the interviewer, 'After the war, my mother never went to church again.' Nicolson quotes another similar comment: 'One woman told the *Gazette*, "I went for a walk last night instead of going to church: I felt it would do me more good."'

There were still celebrations and occasions to mark the achievements of the war effort. Leeds, along with everywhere else, had been asked to raise funds, in all possible ways. There had been Tank Weeks across the country, and savings bonds had been sold. Numerous voluntary groups had devised schemes for raising funds. At the opening of the year, all this had been subsumed into a Thanksgiving Week, and that event in itself raised £4.6 million to pay for the war. In July came a Victory Loan campaign, which gathered almost as much again.

Title page of the Annual Report of the Bramley District Nursing Association, 1919. *Author's collection*

It was universal belief that welcomes home and rituals to mark the return of the fighters had to be done – and with *éclat*. One account explains that in Leeds, 'Men were welcomed home from the war; trophies (including a tank) arrived in the city and were placed on exhibition; questions relating to the training and employment of demobilized soldiers loomed large, and both demanded close consideration.'

Regarding the long aftermath of the war and its long-term effects on the combatants who tried to rebuild their lives, there was the lingering problem of how to help the servicemen, with regard to a whole range of ills and sufferings. One of the first major steps in doing something properly proactive in this respect came with the establishment of the Royal British Legion in 1921. As their current website explains:

> Over 6 million men had served in the war – 725,000 never returned. Of those who came back, 1.75 million had suffered some kind of disability and half of these were permanently disabled. To this figure then had to be added those who depended on those who had gone to war – the wives and children, widows and orphans.

There was a major struggle ahead for the disabled servicemen, and some striking examples of individual survival were in the news. The popular essayist E.V. Lucas wrote about one such instance, that of Georges Scapini, who had lost his sight in the war, and wrote a book about this, *The Apprenticeship of the Night*. Scapini is brutally honest about the situation he and thousands of others were in after the war: 'As the war continued there would be more wounded, more incapacitated, until they, and I with them, would become a public nuisance. Should that be? I at any rate would not be a reproach, a burden to any community; I would do something.' Indeed he did. Lucas points out that Scapini became successful, 'at the age of thirty-four, in the French Chamber of Deputies'.

In Britain, the situation was dire. The Royal British Legion led the way in working to help rehabilitate wounded men, and also those who were tubercular, and there was an interesting Leeds connection here. A group called Industrial Settlements opened a home for the soldiers at Preston Hall, Aylesford, near Maidstone. The press described the place: 'The men are to be trained under qualified experts in high-class horticulture, fruit growing, poultry farming and other open-air industries. The project also includes the immediate establishment of workshops for the training of ex-servicemen in other pursuits suitable to their condition.' The Hall had already been used by the Red Cross as a

I HAVE DREAMED A DREAM

PART I.

THE DREAM.

I HAVE dreamed a dream, and I want you to dream it with me, and perhaps when you and I have dreamed the dream together, you may be, as I am, filled with a great desire for its realization.

It is not a new dream, and it is not one that I alone have dreamed, and the picture it has presented to each dreamer has been moulded and shaped by influences, psychological, temperamental and environmental, and thus is not the same.

As I said, it is not a new dream. Ever since war broke out it has been shaping in my mind, very nebulously at first, and the process of precipitation into something like a definite picture began when I first met a man in the blue suit of suffering, limping along with that look of quiet patience and conscious strength and dignity of purpose, unafraid by the terrors through which he has passed, to which we have all become so sadly familiar.

Now each time I see one of these scarred heroes in the familiar blue suit, or, perhaps more pathetic still, I see the tiny gold stripe on a khaki uniform, fresh, vigorous and definite strokes are traced over nebulous portions of my picture until, after two years and more spent in the drawing of it, its main outlines are complete enough to lay before you.

A page from the magazine of the Preston Hall Rehabilitation Home.
Author's collection

military hospital, specifically as a place of treatment for gassed soldiers.

The land was bought from the Leeds Fireclay Company, who were, in fact, the latest version of the famous Burmantofts Pottery, which was situated just a short walk from St James's Infirmary. It was all part of a national drive to give the wounded and tubercular men some hope, and a chance of earning an income. There was even a co-operative land scheme, and a start was made in that plan by the use of Meathop Flats near Morecambe, where, as one report put it, 'the soil is easy to work and particularly suitable for disabled men who must have light employment in salubrious situations.'

There were, as always in major conflicts, individual heroes and heroines as well as sad tales to tell. Leeds had many, but one – a woman who ranks as the quintessential unsung hero – was Mrs Powell Williams. She had been in charge of the Bandages Section of the Military Hospitals Committee (linked to the Lady Mayoress's Committee), and at her base in Park Row, she and her team had produced 200,000 dressings for the wounded. Her reward was 'a suitable presentation' of a special local award.

For some considerable stretch of time after the Armistice, there were lengthy, tortuous and difficult problems of all kinds. Large numbers of men, from all sides, were still in prison, or on duty, or even languishing still in the hospitals and convalescent homes up and down the country. Some of the stories from this strange limbo-land are highly emotional and even tragic. In many cases, men did not reach home for many months after the end of the war, or after their release from German prisons.

The year brought chaos and needless suffering for many who were caught up in either imprisonment in camps or in demobilization. The return of the British prisoners of war was a special challenge. The historian W.H. Scott explains the situation:

> A task of peculiar interest had to be performed … when the British prisoners of war returned home and were conveyed, with their luggage, to the great camp at Ripon, there to prepare for demobilization. Very expeditiously were they carried to their destination. Many were deeply impressed when they saw the procession of brilliantly lit cars coming to meet them.

The conscientious objectors were still in jail – many still in Wormwood Scrubs. But some were in Wakefield, and the Leeds war resisters had been placed there at one time. One story from this shameful aspect of conscription in the war concerns a Leeds man.

Ernest England was a Quaker from Leeds. Despite being classified as medically unfit for military service, he was not left alone when the Military Service Act came into force in January 1916. He was recalled, and put into army custody. So began a sad tale of mother and son, leading to one of the most inhuman and tragic deaths in the story of resistance to war.

As Ernest was taken to York Barracks, his mother, who had been with him up to that point, was taken ill. A few days later, the son was told that his mother was very seriously ill and was dying. He was given no compassionate leave by the immediate authorities, but a family member took the extreme step of phoning the brigadier general of the regiment, and Ernest was given permission. He was by that time at Ripon Camp, and his only means of getting to Leeds was by taxi. He arrived at his mother's side just a few hours before she passed away. He stayed for her funeral, but then in June 1917 he was sent to Wormwood Scrubs.

Then began his slow decline. Ernest was weak; he had a serious illness himself, but was still put to hard work. He was at the Scrubs, and then transferred to Knutsford, where there was a workshop; but still he was on the move, to Wakefield and then to Dartmoor. The first historian of the No-Conscription Fellowship takes up the story:

> His letters from Dartmoor show him shivering with cold, working in the snow with wet feet, and suffering from the diet ... after a day of hard shovel work, tea consisted of a thick slice of bread, a scrape of margarine and a mug of tea. ... Six weeks later his enfeebled frame succumbed to influenza at home on 6 March 1919.

Ernest's was an extreme case. In most instances, the men who had been hospitalized in the hundreds of military hospitals tended to benefit immeasurably from the *esprit de corps* that was created by patients and staff. All the evidence points to a determined effort to inject humour and distraction for the community in the wards. Some material has survived from these convalescence sites, and in 1918 in particular, they were crucially important for morale, as many of the wounded wanted to be home, and yet were in limbo. One such survival is a cuttings and autograph book from Frickley Hall, near Doncaster, where servicemen from all across the land were cared for. The entries give a close-up profile of the spirit and morale of the men. For instance, Trooper A. Cartwright, of the 5th Army Corps, British Expeditionary Force, provided a sketch of the hall; an anonymous man, who had clearly been to Suez, provided a comic postcard; and E.A. Keel of the Coldstream Guards supplied some lines: *'Look at this page and think of me/when far away perhaps I'll be.'* There is the usual dark humour also, as in

Private P. Cartwright's lines (5th KOYLI, 1914):

Here's health to the Kaiser
The Crown Prince as well.
I wish all Germans were in Germany
And Germany was in ... (well, you know).

The nurse who kept the book was one Nellie Organ, who otherwise would have always been forgotten as one of the many who did that wonderful work. But her book has preserved her name and her picture.

Looking back from the standpoint of 1919 and the year after the Armistice, as far as Leeds is concerned what really stands out is the tremendous effort given to recreation and entertainment. Apart from the professional groups and the in-house hospital assemblies, there was a national movement that had an impact in Leeds, and lasted from 1915 to 1921. This was the Music in War Time concept, whose aims were 'to afford entertainment to soldiers or sailors in camp, hospital or elsewhere' and 'to give professional musicians, hard hit by the war, a little assistance by the payment of modest fees – usually a guinea a concert'. In Leeds, it was Miss Paget and Sydney Nicholson who developed the idea. As usual, there was a committee to handle it, and again it was spawned by the ubiquitous Lady Mayoress's Committee.

The series of concerts started in Cookridge Hospital, and more and

The dining and recreation hall at the VAD hospital, Templenewsam.
Leeds Library

more followed. Scott says that 5,000 fees were paid to musicians in its six years of life. The main audiences were at the major Leeds hospitals and the vast camps at Ripon, where all the Pals were training. Scott wrote, 'Altogether about sixty hospitals in various parts of the county were visited and concerts were organized even as far afield as Clipstone (Nottinghamshire) and Newcastle.'

There was another musical mover and shaker around as well – Percy Scholes. Percy was born in 1877 in Headingley, the third child of Thomas Scholes, a commercial agent. What Percy came to represent was that type that proliferated in the late Victorian and Edwardian years – the autodidact, the self-taught man of letters, or humanist. He was bronchitic all his life, and so his schooling was adversely affected. Consequently, he read widely and at random, although music was always going to be his primary interest. From school to work was hardly what many parents would have wanted for their bookish son, because he started merely as an assistant in the Yorkshire College library. That was later to become the University of Leeds, and it was to be an ambience that suited his disposition. Percy was a lover of theory and history, the writing behind and about music, and with that he began as a teacher, first of all giving lectures on music at Kent College in Canterbury and then abroad in South Africa. That was an extremely enterprising and unusual route to academic status, but such things were possible then before the era of the extreme specialist.

But after that beginning of rather random and vague association with adult education, his career began to take on a more orthodox hue when he gained some qualifications – the ARCM (Associate of the Royal College of Music). Percy achieved this at the same time that he taught at an extension college in Manchester. In fact, as that course was what we now call 'musical appreciation', it explains much about what he wanted to do and where his aims lay.

This more structured academic life was confirmed when he qualified for his Bachelor of Music degree in 1908 at St Edmund Hall, Oxford. He found time to marry in 1908, but was busy doing something truly innovative: he conceived the notion of home study. This had been developed during his time teaching adults in the Co-operative Holidays Association, and it was a step in education that found a ready response. The result was an organization called the Home Study Union.

Percy Scholes became the key figure in the home study field, and he edited the journal *The Music Student* for many years; he also ventured into music writing for the papers, becoming music critic of *The Evening*

Standard for seven years and also writing for *The Queen* magazine. It was not an easy time for him: newly married and with no regular salary, he was existing essentially as a freelancer, but as long as he was prepared to travel around, he had work, because Oxford, Cambridge and London all wanted his lecturing services.

Percy learned by hard experience and could turn his hand to anything within musical studies. He was busy during the Great War and made sure that his expertise was employed in a scheme with the YMCA, with the soldiers as the audience: Music for the Troops. It was inevitable that he would progress in his writing from articles and lesson notes to books. A man with his wide knowledge was ideal as a writer of reference works, and in 1919 he published *A Listener's Guide to Music*. He later wrote the *Oxford Companion to Music* (1938) as well as other books.

What really brought his popularizing talents out was his involvement with the media beyond print; although he became a music critic for *The Observer* in the 1920s, he also found that in broadcasting he could really reach people and educate them in musical knowledge. The natural slot for him was in a weekly talk, printed as well as broadcast, and the *Radio Times* was the perfect organ for this type of dissemination of knowledge. This talent he had for making classical music popular had an impact during the war. In November 1915 he wrote a feature called 'An Appeal to Elgar' in which he asked for a piece that 'should be a choral piece which shall be wide enough in its verbal utterance to express the feelings of us all, something not too difficult for our choral societies'. What he was envisaging, in the time of war, was something like *The Last Night of the Proms*. As part of the Elgar Festival in 1916 there were performances in Leeds and Bradford, and these raised large sums of money for the Red Cross. Scholes was, more than anything, a popularizer of music.

Percy Scholes and Miss Paget, with their cohorts of enthusiasts for a 'good tune', were exactly what was needed in bringing popular classics to the average man in the street (and the Tommies, of course).

But in 1919, when there was at least some attempt to look forward rather than back, there was a realization that there had been a momentous rush of social change as well as a traumatic experience of unprecedented scale. Derek Fraser, writing on post-war Leeds, sums it up as a period when merely partial success had been achieved in some quarters:

> In 1919, Leeds was on the brink of the great changes in civic enterprise and social acceptance that were later taken for granted. Only 50 per cent of the population had the vote. ... For the first

time women had the parliamentary vote, but the 70,000 women under thirty were not enfranchised until 1928. ... The implications of electricity and of the internal combustion engine were beginning to exercise the minds of the city fathers, and the whole question of transport, by road, rail and eventually air, had serious consequences for town planning.

There were great changes ahead, and Leeds, along with the rest of Britain, had to cope with a future that looked bleak. But if we have to look for a symbol of a brighter future, then, in a city crazy for football, why not look at Leeds City Football Club, as it was in 1919? Just before the war, Herbert Chapman, the great manager, was appointed to take charge at Leeds. He signed a very talented player, Jimmy Speirs, in 1912, and Speirs was to have a distinguished army life, winning a Military Medal in the Second Battle of Arras in 1917, after which he became a sergeant. Unfortunately, he was killed at Passchendaele in August that year.

Matters went from bad to worse for Leeds City. The new league season began on 30 August 1919, and the world was rocked by industrial action as readjustments to peace continued. The team had to travel to one match, at Wolves, by charabanc, as there was a rail strike. Things deteriorated for Leeds City with financial troubles, and at the city's Hotel Metropole, players and assets were auctioned off.

However, as all football fans know, the birth of Leeds United was not far away, in the 1920s. In a way peculiarly fitting for the city of Leeds, those problematic few years for Leeds City FC and its rebirth surely reveal some kind of moral tale about the war itself and about the refusal of the human spirit to give in. In a football publication from the 1930s, when Leeds United had arrived, we have a statement that backs this up: 'In the years that have come and gone since its formation the club has had many ups and downs, but the "downs" have been overcome, and Leeds United is now one of the best managed and most successful clubs in the English league.' Many Leeds people would take that as applying to their city generally.

Finally, there is one more very interesting statement from the 1930s' book: 'The man who signs for Leeds United must be a good player and a good citizen; he must be a man who must uphold the dignity of the professional football player.' That sentence has to apply to the people of Leeds in that truly dreadful war as well: they showed the world that they could 'uphold the dignity' of the individual and the family in times of great suffering.

Acknowledgements

Anyone writing on the history of Leeds in the Great War has to give a special note of thanks to two writers in particular: David Thornton and Peter Liddle. The former has provided a solid basis of material for anyone writing about the city, and the latter has provided a most important Great War archive at the University of Leeds. It would not be an exaggeration to say that Dr Liddle has devoted himself to giving the substance of real human experience of war to the historical collection, and he is an enthusiastic advocate of discussion and debate on the war, as typified by his conference 'The First World War in Perspective', held at Weetwood Hall, Leeds, in the summer of 2014.

Thanks also to staff at the Leeds Library, and at the University of Hull, the latter in particular for help with the material on conscientious objection.

An Afterword

When the research for this book began, I saw what seemed to be a clear surface of material: that is, there was a distinct outline of events and a well-established chronology. That is all very useful, but it pertains to the slender exterior only. In between the so-called major events and decisive battles, there is the elusive, intractable human tragedy that permeated every family across the nations and empires that were involved in the war, as the dominoes of events toppled over. I knew at the outset that some of my own ancestors from Leeds were involved, and I thought that perhaps I could locate and understand their experience better than I had ever done before. I was wrong.

This is not said with any sense of failure or defeat. It is intended to confirm what another historian, Keith Jeffrey, once wrote about the challenge of trying to understand events and people from the past. He said the problem was facing 'the mute strangeness of things and the unfathomability of lives past'. I feel that we think like that, even while gazing at the family photographs from that incomprehensible mass conflict.

Yet, as so often when we try to untie the knot of past thinking and feeling, some of the key to real knowledge lies in the archives as well as in the handed-down tales. The latter tend to be half-truths and even sometimes sheer myths, but the solid, documented facts of archival material give us a frisson of pleasure, as they present us with a closeness to those 'unfathomable' lives.

I hope that my quest to reveal the character of my home city in those war years has perhaps given some kind of template for others who might try the same kinds of enquiries. I sense that so many of us, in trying to move closer to 1914, have those persistent memories of silent men and women from that wartime generation, whose silence was a determined attempt to keep the unspeakable unspoken. But now, a century on, those accounts of 'What you did in the war, Dad' and the mysteries of such fragments as 'He never talks about it … it was so awful' may perhaps just evaporate a little in the face of so much resolute determination that so many of us now seem to have – delving into the truths of the first truly world war that humanity knew.

Bibliography and Sources

Note: William Herbert Scott's monumental work *Leeds in the Great War 1914–1918* tells the story of the city in terms of a close-up on officials, civic events and military measures. That has provided a platform. I have also been fortunate in having significant press material. Otherwise, much of the biographical material has been gleaned from obscure memoirs. I have avoided concentrating too much on the material relating to army sources, as others have already done that research in great depth. Anyone writing on Leeds at this period owes a profound debt to Mr Scott. He should be more widely known, and I feel I have done my part in helping to achieve this.

Books cited

Barbellion, W.N.P., *The Journal of a Disappointed Man*, Penguin, London, 1948.

Bennett, Alan, *Writing Home,* Faber & Faber, London, 1994.

Beresford, M.W., *The Leeds Chamber of Commerce*, Leeds Incorporated Chamber of Commerce, 1951.

Brooks, J. Barlow, *Lancashire Bred Part II*, self-published, Oxford, 1950.

Buchan, John, *The Battle of the Somme – First Phase*, Thomas Nelson, London, 1919,

Coates, Ken, *British Labour and the Russian Revolution*, Spokesman Books, Nottingham, 1974.

Davenport-Hines, R.P.T., *Dudley Docker: The Life and Times of a Trade Warrior*, Cambridge University Press, 1984.

Ferguson, Norman, *The First World War: A Miscellany*, Summersdale, London, 2014.

Fiennes, Peter, *To War with God*, Mainstream Publishing, Edinburgh, 2011.

Fraser, Derek, *A History of Modern Leeds*, Manchester University Press, 1980.

Graham, John W., *Conscription and Conscience: A History 1916–1919*, George Allen & Unwin, London, 1922.

Griffin, Stephen, *Ken Dodd: The Biography, Michael O'Mara*, London, 2005.

Halliday, Wilfrid J., *D.U.R. A Memoir*, Brotherton Library, Leeds, 1969.

Johnston, Frank, and Allison, George, *The Football Encyclopaedia*,

Associated Sporting Press, London, 1934.

Losowsky, Monty, (Ed.), *Getting Better: Stories from the History of Medicine*, Medical Museum Publishing, Leeds, 2007.

Lucas. E.V., *Traveller's Luck: Essays and Fantasies*, Methuen, London, 1930.

Newbury, Maggie, *Reminiscences of a Bradford Mill Girl*, City of Bradford Libraries Division, 1980.

Nicolson, Juliet, *The Great Silence*, John Murray, London, 2009.

Price, A.C., *Leeds and its Neighbourhood*, Oxford University Press, 1909.

Priestley, J.B., *Margin Released*, Heinemann, London, 1962.

Ratcliffe, Dorothy Una, *Lady of a Million Daffodils*, Titus Wilson, Kendal, no date.

Scott, William Herbert, *Leeds in the Great War 1914–1918: A Book of Remembrance*, Leeds Library and Arts Committee, 1923.

Stewart, Sheila, *Lifting the Latch*, Oxford University Press, 1964.

Stobart, Mrs St.Clair, *War and Women: from experience in the Balkans and elsewhere*, G.Bell & Sons, London, 1913.

Wall, Max, *The Fool on the Hill*, Quartet Books, London, 1975.

What Happened at Leeds, (a group of *Daily Express* features bound into book form), Pelican Press, London, 1917.

General reference

Brearley, Michael, *The Times One Hundred Greatest Cricketers*, Macmillan, London, 1998.

Cannon, John, *Oxford Dictionary of British History*, Oxford University Press, 2001.

Colls, Robert, and Dodd, Philip, (Eds.), *Englishness, Politics and Culture 1880–1920*, Bloomsbury, London, 1986.

Foster, D.B., *Leeds Slumdom*, C.H. Halliday, Leeds, 1897.

Griffiths, Gareth, *Women's Factory Work in World War I*, Alan Sutton, Stroud, 1991.

Heinrich, Anselm, *Entertainment, Propaganda, Education: Regional Theatre in Germany and Britain between 1918 and 1945*, University of Hertfordshire Press/Society for Theatre Research, 2007.

Hollis, Matthew, *Now All Roads Lead to France*, Faber & Faber, London, 2011.

Howse, Christopher (Ed.), *How We Saw It: 150 Years of the Daily Telegraph*, Ebury Press, London, 2005.

Kerr, Gordon, *A Short History of the First World War*, Oldcastle Books, Harpenden, 2014.

1914 in Yorkshire, York Museums Trust, 2014.

Liddington, Jill, *Rebel Girls: How votes for women changed Edwardian lives*, Virago, London, 2006.

McConnell, James, *Recollections of the Great War in the Air*, Pen & Sword, Barnsley, 2013.

Pollock, Margaret A. (Ed), *Working Days: being the personal records of sixteen working men and women*, Jonathan Cape, London, 1926.

Potter, Harry, *Law, Liberty and the Constitution*, Boydell Press, Woodbridge, 2015.

Pratt, Edwin A., *Railways and the Great War*, Selwyn & Blount, London, 1921.

Russell, Bertrand, *The Autobiography of Bertrand Russell Vol. 2*, Allen & Unwin, London, 1968.

Sandford, Christopher, *The Final Over: The Cricketers of Summer, 1914*, The History Press, Stroud, 2014.

Saunders, John B., *Mozley and Whiteley's Law Dictionary*, Butterworth's, London, 1977.

The Stage Year Book, The Stage Offices, London, 1914.

Thornton, David, *Leeds: A Historical Dictionary of People, Places and Events*, Northern Heritage Publications, Huddersfield, 2013.

The Times Digital Archive

'Economy Hints for Housekeepers', 6 July 1915, reprinted 6 July 2015.

'The Production of Munitions', 10 June 1915, p. 9, issue 40877.

'Tubercular Ex-Servicemen', 16 March 1920, p. 13, issue 42360.

'Work for Disabled Men', 4 April 1919, p. 14, issue 42066.

Essays and articles

Reeve, Noel, 'Legacies of War', in www.arts.leeds.ac.uk: 'A Leeds Woman's Story: The British War Graves Association'.

Rowley, Tom, 'The Cricketers who fought for their country in World War One', *Daily Telegraph* online 2015.

Sheffield, Gary, 'The Centenary of the First World War: An unpopular view, *The Historian*, Summer 2014, pp. 22–26.

Thornton, David, 'Leeds and the First World War', Publications of the Thoresby Society, Second Series, Vol. 24, *Miscellany*, 2013, pp. 111–134.

Waddington, Keir, '"We don't want any German sausages here!", Food, Fear and the German Nation in Victorian and Edwardian Britain', *Journal of British Studies*, Vol. 52, issue 4, October 2013, pp. 1017-1042.

Newspapers and periodicals

References made to features in the *Leeds Mercury*, *The Yorkshire Post* and the *Yorkshire Evening News* – all sourced from the archive at the Leeds Central Library. Also, extracts have been used from *The Times Digital Archive* (listed above).

Other archival sources

Album: Fryston Hall convalescence home, 1914–18, author's collection.
Hansard, 6 July 1915, Vol. 73, cc 185–7, 'Alien Enemies'.
Unpublished material from Percy Sykes, conscientious objector, author's collection.

Online resources

www.invisionzone.com/greatwarforum
www.leeds.gov.uk/libraries
www.leodis.net
www.leodis.net/playbills
www.leodis.net/discovery

INDEX